LICKIN' THE BEATERS 2

Vegan Chocolate and Candy

ILLUSTRATED BY
CELSO & MISSY KULIK

SIUE MOFFAT

LICKIN' THE BEATERS 2

Vegan Chocolate and Candy

ILLUSTRATED BY CELSO & MISSY KULIK

SIUE MOFFAT

"Lickin' the Beaters 2 *is not for the faint of heart!*
Are you afraid of sugar and fat? Then don't buy this book!
For those who like their vegan desserts sweet and rich, I dare
you to bake and boil until your house smells like a chocolate
factory and your friends come banging on your door."

— CHAD MILLER, *Food Fight Vegan Grocery* —

LICKIN' THE BEATERS 2 *Vegan Chocolate and Candy*

By Siue Moffat

ISBN: 978–1–60486–009–2
Library Of Congress Control Number: 2008906337
Copyright © 2011 Siue Moffat
All artwork copyright individual artists and used by kind permission.
This edition copyright © 2011 PM Press
All Rights Reserved

PM Press
PO Box 23912
Oakland, CA 94623
www.pmpress.org
Illustrations by Celso & Missy Kulik
Designed by Courtney Utt and Tofu Hound Press

Printed in the USA on recycled paper.

Table of Contents

Ice Creem

Angels and Devils:
The Duality of Dessert

*i*t seems the best things in life are both wonderful and awful at the same time. Think sex, drugs, and rock 'n' roll (or sex, dessert, and punk rock). For every good element you can think of there is a bad element as well. Sugar and chocolate are no different.

My first book, *Lickin' the Beaters: Low Fat Vegan Desserts*, was for the most part healthier than sweets you would buy off the shelf — whole grain flours, low fat, and less sugar. My philosophy concerning desserts then was, "If it's healthy–ish you can eat as much as you want!" I think this is a good philosophy. As I was nearing the end of that book, however, I began thinking of this book — the decadence to end all vegan decadence — sugar and chocolate. With no holds barred I began concocting sugary delights that would satisfy any (and possibly only) twelve-year-old sweet-teeth. I decided this end of the spectrum was an interesting counterpoint.

In the middle of testing recipes for the first book it became clear that I was probably addicted to sugar and that perhaps some of my health problems were caused or aggravated by it. Interestingly, this did not stop me from going through with this new book, it just made me think more about this duality of dessert.

Most people know the angelic qualities of sugar and chocolate. They make you feel good, they put smiles on people's faces, they encourage social interaction and sharing, they give you a burst of energy, they can be used as ingredients for gastronomic art, and looking at them in a scientific sphere, they are quite remarkable.

Chocolate, although strictly controlled by scientists in these modern times, still needs masterful skill and knowledge to go from plant to bar. The cacao trees grow within twenty degrees of the equator where the temperature never dips below sixty degrees. The young trees first grow in the shadows of tall hardwoods, then as they age they need more sun. They are pollinated by a small midge (fly) that lives in the underbrush. The cacao pods have forty beans. The pods are split with machetes, the beans and white pulp are fermented in banana leaves for about a week. Afterwards the beans are dried in the sun for up to nine days. If one bean goes bad it can spoil the whole bunch. After roasting the beans are broken into nibs — this is the purest form of chocolate consumers can buy. The nibs are ground and heated to become chocolate liquor. The liquor is separated into cocoa butter and cocoa powder. The liquor is then mixed with sugar and some cocoa butter to produce chocolate as we know it.

Drinking chocolate has been around for thousands of years. It wasn't until 1692 that English pubs offered edible chocolate bars. It wasn't until 1872 that milk was added.

A 1991 study concluded that 50 percent of all food cravings were for chocolate, and 40 to 50 percent of women crave it. Some possible reasons are that chocolate melts at body temperature — there are very few room temperature foods that melt in your mouth. Also, eating chocolate releases serotonin and dopamine in the brain, giving a happy feeling, much like many illegal drugs. In the United States 2.8 billion pounds of chocolate are consumed each year.

And sugar — what other kind of food can you think of that has so many different shapes, sizes, textures, colors? A rise or fall of temperature can create an entirely new food. Mixing or not mixing, at any given time, produces a different treat.

The sugar cane stalk is refined, at one time with the use of animal blood, to produce crystallized sugar as we know it. Today many sugar companies use animal bones in the refining process to whiten the sugar — this is why the term "vegan sugar" is used to refer to those products that are processed without bones. During processing the molasses is removed to make the product whiter. Regular brown sugar is white sugar with some molasses added. Vegan sugar that is less processed has more molasses naturally occurring. Sugar also comes from sugar beets, used primarily in North America, Europe, and Russia, but this form only takes up 30 percent of the sugar market.

Sugar's history is long, although honey, dates, unrefined sugar cane, and other naturally sweet whole foods were around thousands of years before the refining of sugar cane. As soon as we figured out this process, however, our appetite for the granular whiteness soared. In the mid-1300s sugar was not consumed in England. In 1662 it was consumed at 16 million pounds a year. In the 1880s Americans consumed forty-eight pounds of sugar per person per year. By 2000 it had risen to 160 pounds.

Sugar is 100 percent sweet — it affects only the sweet buds on our tongue. Babies and children immediately take a liking to sweetness as soon as they have their first taste. For some people, this is the start of their lifelong commitment to dessert. Many chefs will tell you their secret ingredient is sugar — they put a little bit in virtually every dish they make. It's clear — we love the stuff.

So what are some of the less angelic qualities of sugar and chocolate? It's something that affluent people in the West don't think too much about. It's important to know where your food comes from and how it gets onto your plate, whether it be knowledge of factory farming or vegetation.

Labor Issues

Chocolate and sugar industries have awful records regarding human rights. Sugar was the main crop that fueled the huge grotesque slavery machine. Africans were brought to cane fields in Brazil and the Caribbean — many countries originally involved included Spain, Great Britain, Portugal, France, and the Netherlands. Americans also took part in this human rights atrocity, as we all know.

Chocolate production has recently been targeted for child labor abuses. Most cacao farms are actually owned by families, but because the market pushes the price down they often take others' children into their house to harvest the plants. Children are tricked or sold into servitude when they are as young as nine years old. There is said to be as many as fifteen thousand children currently working in chocolate production. Farmers, if they are lucky, make one-hundredth the price of what a high-end chocolate bar sells for in North America. Even with the massive amounts of pesticides putting workers' heath in danger, 21 percent of crops are lost to disease and 25 percent are lost to pests.

Some experts have stated that sugar work is the most perilous in America. In Florida, a modern sugar bowl, poverty and sugar go hand-in-hand. Workers, mostly from Central America, still struggle for fair wages as they did decades before.

Racism

Obviously slavery is linked to racism. The sugar colonialists would pack the Africans into the ships like sardines — there was a 13 percent mortality rate. A ship of slaves could bring sixty thousand pounds sterling. There was smallpox and dysentery. Some slaves committed suicide. Some went on hunger strikes and were force fed. There was torture — nailing limbs to sticks and burning the sticks, whipping and applying salt to the wounds. All were branded.

Originally Queen Elizabeth I was appalled at the idea of forcing Africans from their country to work without pay in sugar plantations. But when the money rolled in from the first bounty of slave labor, she gave the second voyage of colonists a ship and took shares.

The clergy were more interested in "saving souls" than banishing slavery. The French in Haiti took slave mistresses. These children were often shipped to France for education, but when they returned they still did not have rights.

The sugar fields in Hawaii were first cleared by Chinese workers. "Black–birding" or "Shanghai–ing" is often mentioned in the history of Hawaiian sugar labor. Men were fed alcohol and woke up to find themselves on a ship heading for the American territory. Soon, the mainland Americans thought there were too many Chinese people immigrating to the country and Congress banned Chinese labor, which filtered down to the islands. This then happened with Japanese people, followed by Filipinos.

Both chocolate and sugar farmers, while clearing out brush and making the land plantable, also continued to "clear out" indigenous people. Originally, the Spanish tried to enslave the Arawak Indians (who were vegetarian, incidentally) to work the fields in Haiti and Dominican Republic,

but instead wiped out the whole race. The peace-loving, mild–mannered Arawak could not take the back-breaking labor and constant cruel punishment.

Environmental Damage

Both chocolate and sugar tend to be monocrops that take over an area. In Hawaii in 1915, 90 percent of the agriculture was sugar. This causes numerous problems including the leaching of nutrients from the soil and increasing pests, thereby increasing the use of pesticides. Pesticides often run off into other plots of land and water tables.

When growing sugar cane, huge tracts of land must be cleared and irrigated. Two hundred pounds of water are needed to produce half a pound of sugar. While in some areas locals might consider irrigation "beautifying" to an area that might have been mostly scrub brush, this causes hundreds of animal species and vegetation varieties to become instinct. The construction of the irrigation system itself disrupts the environment. Ecosystems are demolished.

Big Business

From the beginning, sugar's history has been clouded in lies and greediness. As humans consumed more sugar, they became sicker. Some early physicians made the link, and in return they were called witches and sorcerers. Quack doctors were bleeding people and other such bizarre things in order not to implicate sugar in diseases. Scientists pinned down diabetes in the 1500s but the Latin word "mellitus" was added at the end — "mel" meaning honey — in the 1770s. In modern times, when the World Health Organization proclaimed that sugar should only consist of 10 percent or less of a healthy diet, the industry came out baring their teeth; they insisted 25 percent was healthy.

The chocolate industry also manipulates through marketing and propaganda. During the early 1970s, Americans were more health-conscious and ate less sweets. Mars Corporation came out with ads equating one of their top chocolate bars with drinking a glass of milk. (They got in trouble with that ad, something that probably wouldn't happen today. We vegans might snidely agree, however, that milk *is* as non–beneficial to human health as candy!) In 1984 Mars Corporation paid $5 million to be the official sponsor of the Olympics. This chocolate company also fronted a misleading dental research clinic that provided free literature for waiting rooms in dental offices. The articles were praising the "wonderful healthful qualities" of milk chocolate.

In the 1990s, the Chocolate Manufacturing Association, National Candy Brokers Association, and National Confectioners Association put pressure on Congress to extend Daylight Savings Time through November to give an extra hour of daylight to trick-or-treaters! We saw this change finally come to pass in 2007.

Just as chocolate and sugar's history is plagued with racism and labor troubles, the industry today is equally guilty of spending lots of time and money deceiving the public.

Health

This is where chocolate and sugar say goodbye to each other and one takes the high road and the other takes the low road. Chocolate, as it turns out, really isn't bad for you. It actually has several properties that are beneficial including being high in antioxidants. There are many studies proving cacao can help lower blood pressure and help with asthma. Why chocolate gets a bad rap is wholly the fault of his friend sugar, and also our enemy milk. All the studies showing that chocolate is fattening and causes acne and tooth decay were done on milk chocolate bars (or "candy bars"), which are about half sugar. Premium dark chocolate has fat that is partially oleic acid — the same good fat in olive oil. The fat in chocolate, cocoa butter, does not raise cholesterol like animal fats do. Premium dark chocolate is lower in sugar, as it has 63 percent or more cocoa solids. Fifty grams of this kind of bar will have about ten grams of sugar. Fifty grams of a standard milk chocolate bar has twenty grams of sugar. A typical "candy bar," which contains additions like peanuts and caramel, has an average of twenty-six grams of sugar per fifty-gram bar.

What is it about sugar that makes it so devilish? Everything nutritious that was in the sugarcane has been stripped away. Sugar is probably the most refined food on the planet. Cane sugar is mostly sucrose, which breaks down into glucose and fructose upon digestion. These sugars go rapidly into the bloodstream where they raise blood glucose levels. Before the sugar intake our bodies are balanced. When sugar is introduced, our pancreas hurries to push down the amount of glucose in the blood, while the adrenal glands fight to do their job — push it back up. An unbalance in this system is basically what diabetes is all about.

Excess sugar is stored in the liver as glycogen. When it has reached its limit the liver processes the excess glycogen into fatty acids that are stored in places like thighs and waists, then moves onto more serious places like the kidneys and the heart. Functioning of all these systems is weakened. Some studies link sugar with cancer (as it weakens the immune system), and dementia (for the brain needs a steady supply of glucose and the teeter-totter effect is dangerous). Excess sugar has proven to be the cause of tooth decay. It is thought to be a primary contributor to candida — yeast overgrowth. Practically the only way to deal with candida is to cut out sugar entirely — even fruit and sugar alcohols like sorbitol (which diabetes sufferers can use). Candida causes migraines, fatigue, joint pain, endometriosis, acid reflux, dental infections, depression, panic attacks, etc.

To put sugar in perspective, the USDA, a conservative government organization that suggests eating red meat and dairy products every day, says you shouldn't eat more than forty grams (ten teaspoons) of sugar a day in a 2,200-calorie diet. Even if you don't eat a candy bar a day chances are you are far exceeding your sugar limit due to the fact that sugar is in almost all processed foods. In Canada the "Food Pyramid" suggests a limit of two teaspoons of sugar a day.

In everyday life the pros of dessert are pretty visible — there just isn't another food that can put a huge smile on any human being's face. Desserts make us giddy and bring us back to childhood; they are always associated with good things. (I acknowledge this and feel it too, sometimes more than most!) I also think we should acknowledge the history and problems with food in Western society. We gorge and glut on sweets without thinking. When you are making recipes from this book take a little time to ponder your situation and impact in the world. Make your desserts really cruelty free; buying local organic and fair trade ingredients will benefit people, animals, and environments all over this planet.

Here is a short list of some fair trade chocolate and sugar manufacturers. They have vegan products, and some are also organic. This isn't a complete list, and I've purposely not included large corporations as they tend to have only one or two bars that use fair trade ingredients, instead of taking the lead and manufacturing all their chocolate with them:

Cocoa Camino
www.cocoacamino.com

Equal Exchange sugar and chocolate
www.equalexchange.coop

Equita sugar, chocolate, spices, rice
www.shopequita.com/food.htm

Divine Chocolate
www.divinechocolate.com

Art Bars
ithacafinechocolates.stores.yahoo.net

Sweet Earth Chocolates
www.sweetearthchocolates.com

Theo Chocolate
www.theochocolate.com

Wholesome Sweeteners
www.wholesomesweeteners.com

Chocolate Santander
www.chocolatesantander.com
(Single origin chocolate — not Fair Trade Certified but seem to have good business practices. Plus the bars are nothing short of amazing.)

Terra Nostra
www.terranostrachocolate.com
(Not Fair Trade Certified, but they do seem very concerned with the issues. Their rice milk chocolate bar is really great and in my opinion is the best 'vegan milk' chocolate bar out there.)

Bibliography

Ballinger, Roy A. *A History of Sugar Marketing.* Washington, D.C.: U.S. Department of Agriculture, 1971.

Coe, Sophie D. and Michael D. *The True History of Chocolate.* London: Thames & Hudson, 1996.

Dufty, William. *Sugar Blues.* New York: Warner Books, 1975.

Equita Fair Trade: www.equita.qc.ca

Macinnis, Peter. *Bittersweet: the Story of Sugar.* Crows Nest, NSW: Allen & Unwin, 2002.

Mintz, Sidney W. *Sweetness and Power: The Place of Sugar in Modern History.* New York: Penguin Books, 1985.

Paquette, Robert L. *Sugar Is Made with Blood: The Conspiracy of La Escalera and the Conflict Between Empires over Slavery in Cuba.* Middletown, Conn.: Wesleyan University Press, 1988.

Pottker, Jan. *Crisis in Candyland: Melting the Chocolate Shell of the Mars Family Empire.* Bethesda, Md.: National Press Books, 1995.

Richardson, Tim. *Sweets: A History of Candy.* New York: Bloomsbury, 2002.

TransFair USA: www.transfairusa.org

Tucker, Richard P. *Insatiable Appetite: The United States and the Ecological Degradation of the Tropical World.* Berkeley: University of California Press, 2000.

Acknowledgments

Special Thanks to YOU, who have waited seven years for this book.

Big Thanks to all my guinea pigs — those of you who willingly or unknowingly tested my recipes for me and allowed me to hog the kitchen. Among them — the old Microcosm house, Food Fight Vegan Grocery, The Ranch, Michele and Sarah D, Grace Street, Liberty Hall, and my family.

Super Thanks to Missy and Celso — the most patient and talented artists a cookbook writer could ever hope for. Please look them up: www.missykulik.com, celso333@hotmail.com.

Thumbs up to all the contributing chefs. Please check out their websites because their food is amazing!

Gratitude to PM Press/Tofu Hound Press who actually made this happen. It was certainly a long journey!

Hugs to my parents for helping me with the green.

Three kisses to Margarita for her hard work with a ridiculous deadline!

Thank you to Timothy and Suzanne's Specialties who gave me amazing products to use in during my testing. I don't see any other company making vegan marshmallow fluff, do you? www.suzannes-specialties.com

Thanks to everyone not mentioned above who helped me, supported me, ate my weird candy with a smile, sent me messages and patiently waited for this book. You inspired me to take a chance and start a vegan chocolate business — Boardwalk Chocolates.

This book is dedicated to those who go above and beyond animal rights. I give my deep respect for all of you who draw the links between different oppressions and fight to make this a cruelty-free world on all levels. You're really making a difference!

A list of things that fueled this book:

Portland: Tragedy, Proper Eats, Food Fight, Sweet Pea Bakery, Brick Wall Records, Coda, Seaside, Oregon, zines and books from Microcosm Publishing, Oaks Park, KBOO Community Radio.

Other: Equalizing Distort on CIUT radio, my bikes: BFI, Pipa (I hope you are in a good home), Stanley, Steckler, Stella and Ms. Steckler, Coast to Coast radio, George Eastman House, my father's Pentax, the stack of old fashioned candy books, Joe Ollmann's books, comics, and animation, Magic Oven Pizza and Panacea Eco Shop in Toronto, Amtrak/VIA, Vegan Treats in PA/NYC, Jonathan's bed time stories.

What Does It Mean?

AGAR aka Agar Agar. Vegan gelatin. Available in powder, flakes, or bar form. Powder is more widely available, so all recipes in this book are made with agar powder. 1 teaspoon of agar powder = 1 tablespoon agar flakes. The powder can be found in health food stores and Asian markets (sometimes it is mixed with sugar — make sure to get the pure stuff), and the flakes can be found in health food stores. The powder dissolves almost instantly and doesn't require very much simmering, whereas the flakes need to be soaked for 15 minutes in the liquid and then simmered for about 15 minutes to ensure dissolving.

AGAVE A very nice sweetener from the agave plant that is often used in sweetening raw or "live" food. It can be used to replace Just Like Honey. It comes in "light," "amber," "blue," and "raw." My favorite is raw amber.

ARROWROOT aka arrowroot starch. You can use this instead of cornstarch. Arrowroot is better because it is less refined and it doesn't need to be cooked as long as cornstarch (overcooking actually weakens it). Once your sauce gets thick it's ready to go — making arrowroot a quick way to thicken liquid.

BARLEY MALT POWDER Often called "malt powder." This is the distinct flavor in nougat chocolate bars and malted milk balls. It's great to add to beverages, cakes, and cookies. The powder is hard to find, but it is available online.

BARLEY MALT SYRUP Often called "malt syrup." This is easily found in health food stores. It is also surprisingly bitter. I prefer using the powder, but it is more difficult to find.

COCOA There are two types: regular ("low fat") and Dutch. The Dutch cocoa is darker and richer. You can use either unless specified. There's a difference between the two, but I like to keep it simple. Remember to always sift it before adding to a recipe.

COCONUT Use unsweetened coconut unless otherwise specified. Sweetened coconut is not only sweeter but moister. Unsweetened coconut is cheaper and easier to find in Canada. If it is not available in grocery stores, it will be available at health food stores.

CORN SYRUP In the United States you can buy it "light" or "dark." Use the light colored unless specified otherwise. In Canada corn syrup is mostly a honey color as this is how the Brits eat it. Corn Syrup is very refined so you can experiment using agave, maple, or rice syrup in its place if you don't want it in your diet.

CUSTARD POWDER This is an English and Canadian thing. It is simply starches and flavor to which you add your own soymilk and sugar. You can find it in specialty food shops in the United States. It's great for filling doughnuts!

EGG REPLACER "Egg replacer" means "dry egg replacer starch" — the kind you get out of a box and mix with water. There are a couple companies that make this stuff. It's a little on the expensive side, so I try to use ground flaxseed when I'm making up a recipe or veganizing one.

EXTRACTS AND FLAVORS For the most part you'll be using typical extracts found in grocery stores that are either flavors based in alcohol or glycerin. Try to use only natural extracts. If you're making high-temperature candy like hard candy, only flavor *oils* will work. Don't mix up extracts and oils when following a recipe as the oils are much more potent than the extracts. You can find oil–based flavors at specialty stores and better supermarkets. Don't use essential oils for cooking or baking.

FLOUR You can use just about any flour in a recipe. Consistency will vary with what you choose, of course. Most of these recipes use regular white unbleached flour. With some recipes, I purposely used and stated non–wheat flour because it's nice to give wheat intolerance people props. Substitute regular wheat flour if you'd like, though if you do, you'll probably have to cut down on the liquids in the recipe.

GRAHAM CRACKERS It is very hard to find these without honey. If you are boycotting honey, I've found animal crackers work really well. There's even a wheat–free brand that has molasses in it so they take on a graham cracker flavor. They also grind well for making crusts.

ICING SUGAR aka confectioners sugar or powdered sugar (which *is* actually different but not to the minds of most people in North America). When I wrote my first book it was impossible to find this unrefined so I barely used it. Nowadays several different companies are making unrefined organic fair trade icing sugar, so I have been using it liberally. You can also make your own (page 122) although it's not quite the same. Always sift before using.

JUST LIKE HONEY This is another amazing product from Suzanne's — the folks who bring you Ricemellow Creme. Available at finer health food stores, this syrup is shockingly like honey — but without the maltreatment of bees! If you can't find Just Like Honey, amber agave syrup will do. *www.suzannes–specialties.com*

MAPLE SYRUP Only buy pure maple syrup; any other "table syrups" are just nasty.

MARGARINE There are numerous unhydrogenated vegan margarines on the market now. Look in your grocer's health food section. Margarine tubs and sticks are both good. Organic shortening, made of palm oil, is good for icings but not so good in baked goods. Cookies are best made with firmer margarine rather than soft margarine.

MOLASSES This is what is extracted when sugar is refined. Do not interchange "Blackstrap" with "Fancy" / "Barbados" in recipes unless specified. The former is actually quite bitter, although it has much more vitamins and minerals.

OIL The best oil to use is sunflower or safflower oil. Soybean and canola oils (aka "vegetable oil") are most likely genetically modified. Not only that, canola, which has been the shining diamond of cooking oils since the late 1980s, is rather controversial as it is derived from the rapeseed plant which has a disconcerting history. You can also try "light" olive oil ("light" refers to the flavor, not the amount of fat).

RICE SYRUP Can be found in health food stores. It is not as sweet as and much thicker than maple syrup.

RICEMELLOW CREME The only marketed vegan marshmallow fluff. A sweet, sticky, airy white goo — it will make your dreams of Fluffer Nutter Sandwiches come true again. Available at finer health food stores. *www.suzannes-specialties.com*

SEMISWEET CHOCOLATE In this collection of recipes "chocolate" and "chocolate chips" automatically mean semisweet unless otherwise noted. Nondairy semisweet is found more easily in common grocery stores in Canada than in the USA. Common semisweet is made with refined sugar, so it may or may not be truly vegan. Luckily there are lots of companies making chocolate bars without refined sugar and these can be chopped up to the size you need. Virtually all vegan bars are semisweet.

SOYMILK You can use whatever nondairy beverage you like. I use vanilla flavor when doing desserts. If you want to make recipes a tad less sweet, use unsweetened soymilk.

SOYMILK POWDER Most soymilk powder is actually defatted soy flour. There are some more expensive kinds of "alternative milk" that have sugar and other flavorings added, and these are much less "beany" than the cheaper stuff. You might need to add a bit more to get a similar thickness.

STEVIA A leaf that is sweet (no sugar what-soever). It is shockingly sweet, so a teaspoon will sweeten a whole cake. Good for diabetics and people avoiding sugar as there is no fructose or glucose in it. Even works with people on candida/yeast overgrowth diets! There are 3 (or more) forms of stevia: green leaf herb, white powder, and liquid. I prefer the liquid because it has less of an aftertaste than the powder and no herby taste of the green leaf. Available in health food stores and some grocery stores, either in the sweetener section or the herbal section.

SUGAR If unspecified it means whatever type of dry vegan sweetener you'd like. "White Sugar" means organic or raw or turbinado ("unrefined") sugar. When making candy use organic sugar — or any other fine unrefined sugar. This is important for melting quickly. "Brown Sugar" means demerara ("unrefined brown") sugar. Use a finer demerara when candy making. Regular white sugar often uses animal bones in the refining process. Regular brown sugar is just refined white sugar with molasses added.

TOFU Please take care you use the right kind! If it doesn't specify, you can use firm/regular or soft. Usually silken firm tofu is the way to go, as opposed to regular firm tofu which can be gritty. Don't use extra firm or you will be very unhappy!

UNSWEETENED CHOCOLATE Usually comes in baking bars of 1 ounce or ½ ounce each. When starting this book nondairy unsweetened chocolate was easy to find, but upon finishing it I've noticed companies putting milk fat into previously dairy-free products! This is highly annoying and anger- inducing! If you can't find vegan unsweetened chocolate, I suggest using vegan semisweet and cutting back on the sugar in the recipe.

WHITE CHOCOLATE Like vegan marshmallows this is an area that needs more experimentation and marketed products. White chocolate isn't really chocolate — it is cocoa butter, sugar, milk products, and sometimes hydrogenated oil. I would have liked to have had some recipes with white chocolate because I love the stuff, but it is extremely hard to find and you would most likely have to purchase it online.

Candy Hints

Candy is scientific. People say that about baking, but I think it's paranoia! Candy making, on the other hand, takes time and requires you to be very patient and follow steps precisely.

✿ If you are in a hurry, don't attempt to make any candy that requires a thermometer.

✿ Heavy-bottom pots are required. If you use cheap aluminum pans I can almost guarantee your candy will burn.

✿ Always use wooden spoons to stir.

✿ Nonstick pans can be used, but because of toxins I prefer stainless steel. Professional candy makers often use pots made of copper.

✿ Most candy is affected badly by heat and humidity in the air — try to keep your candy making restricted to dry 60–65° F weather. If it's raining or snowing out you might have to boil the candy a few degrees higher.

✿ Most candy is supposed to be smooth — this means removing sugar crystals that form on the sides of the pot when you are cooking. Use a damp pasty brush or, if you have to, a fork covered in a damp paper towel. Some recipes require the crystal removal more than others. I've made notes in the recipes that need it.

✿ Most candy requires a low temperature. If you try and rush it you'll end up scorching your candy or having it bubble over. Bad for your morale and bad for the pan and stovetop!

✿ If you have problems with "fat separation" in certain recipes (the sugar and margarine aren't incorporated and candy looks oily) you can add a little hot water to bring the sugar and margarine back together. Add just a little at a time and stir, no more than two tablespoons.

✿ Think of a "plan B" in case you screw up. Would it make a nice icing? Could it be syrup on top of ice creem? Maybe you can crush the candy and put in cookies or on truffles.

✿ Hard candy reacts badly in humid weather, so it is best to wrap each piece individually and store in an airtight container at room temperature. Candy usually lasts for months this way.

✿ Most candy can live in the cool environment of the fridge. I've noted recipes where this isn't the case. Thawing to room temperature will make a nicer eating experience. In any case, all candy needs to be stored in airtight containers.

✿ It's a good idea to soak your pots in hot soapy water immediately after making candy. It saves a cleanup headache afterwards.

Cold Water Test: If you are making candy without a thermometer (heaven forbid!) you can do the "Cold Water Test" to see if your syrup is the consistency you need. Many candy makers use both the thermometer and Cold Water Test together. Drop ½ teaspoon hot syrup from a spoon into a very cold glass of water. Let stand one minute. Take out the syrup ball and examine it.

Soft Ball: Syrup makes a soft ball that doesn't hold its shape. (232° to 240° F)

Firm Ball: Syrup makes a firm ball that holds its shape when held between your fingers. (242° to 248° F)

Hard Ball: Syrup makes a hard ball. Very firm between your fingers, but still pliable. (250° to 268° F)

Soft Crack: Syrup makes a very hard ball that is not pliable (270° to 290° F)

Hard Crack: Syrup is brittle and breaks between your fingers. (300° to 310° F)

Honee Peanut Centers

YIELD: ABOUT 100 SMALL SQUARES

¼ cup margarine
⅓ cup natural peanut butter
pinch of salt
½ cup Just Like Honey
1 tablespoon water
1 teaspoon vanilla
3 cups icing sugar
⅓ cup soymilk powder

1. Grease two 8–inch pans.
2. Combine the margarine, peanut butter, and salt in a pot, mixing on low heat. When the margarine is melted add Just Like Honey, water, and vanilla, and mix well.
3. Put the icing sugar and soy milk powder into a sifter. Gradually sift into peanut mixture. Make candy into a smooth dough–like ball and press into the pan. Cool and cut into small squares for dipping.

Sweet Pecan Centers

YIELD: 8–INCH PAN

1 cup brown sugar, packed
¼ cups margarine
3 tablespoons soymilk
2 cups sifted icing sugar
⅓ cup chopped pecans
1 teaspoon vanilla

1. Grease an 8–inch pan. In a medium pot boil the brown sugar, soymilk, and margarine, stirring constantly.
2. Simmer for about 5 minutes and then stir in the icing sugar, pecans, and vanilla. Pour into pan and place in fridge. Cut into squares when set.

Flavored Marzipan Centers

YIELD: ABOUT 50 PIECES

1 package (7 ounces or 200 grams) of vegan marzipan (almond paste and sugar)
various natural flavorings (such as maple, vanilla, cherry, orange, banana, etc.)

1. Break apart the marzipan and knead a little. Add different flavorings to different parts. Flavorings with a base of oil or glycerine only need one drop per tablespoon of marzipan. Flavorings with a base of alcohol will need more.
2. Mix the flavorings in with your fingers and form into little bite size balls to be dipped.

Coconut Cherry Cream Centers

YIELD: ABOUT 50 PIECES

1 tub (8 ounces) tofu cream cheese
12 tablespoons icing sugar
½ cup finely shredded coconut
½ teaspoon natural cherry extract

1. In a medium pot on medium heat cook all until thickened.
2. Cool. Form into small balls.

Peanut Butter Centers

¼ cup natural peanut butter
dash of salt
icing sugar

1. Melt the peanut butter and salt.
2. Add enough icing sugar to get a soft center that holds its shape.

Lollipops

YIELD: 15 LARGE LOLLIPOPS

Pastry brush
Thermometer

15 lollipop sticks
1 cup sugar
½ cup water
⅓ cup corn syrup
dash of salt
¼ teaspoon natural oil flavoring
(ie. lemon, orange, peppermint, anise)

1. Set lollipop sticks on greased cookie tins or aluminum foil, 4 inches apart.
2. Combine sugar, water, corn syrup, and salt in heavy-bottom pot and place over medium heat, stirring constantly.
3. When the mixture begins to boil remove from heat, cover with tight-fitting lid, and let sit for 3 minutes.
4. Return to heat and bring to boil, without stirring. If sugar crystals form on the sides, wash them down with a wet pastry brush. When mixture reaches 305° F remove from heat and stir in flavoring.
5. Let sit for a few minutes. As the syrup thickens, it makes it easier to pour nice circles. Don't walk away and do something else — waiting too long will cause the syrup to harden in the pot!
6. Pour the syrup with a spoon over the top of the sticks. Wait a few minutes as the candy becomes firm. Unstick the lollipops with a spatula before they cool completely. Be careful! Too much pressure on one side and your sucker will break, sucker! Once cool put in mini plastic bags or wrap in wax paper. If you leave them out too long, they will become sticky.

Words of warning — do not scrape the last bits out of the pot! This will cause your pops to become grainy and not so wonderfully sparklingly clear. Whatever you do, do not boil on high temp or go above 305° F. Your pops will probably begin to scorch and then you've wasted your time!

Fancy Fudge

YIELD: 8–INCH PAN

*A really nice, smooth, rich fudge. If you want a more traditional
fudge, eliminate the cardamom and almond extract.*

Thermometer

3 ounces unsweetened chocolate
½ cup semisweet chocolate chips
⅓ cup Ricemellow Creme
1 teaspoon vanilla extract
½ teaspoon almond extract
1½ cups sugar
1⅓ cups almond soymilk or almond milk
6 tablespoons margarine
1 teaspoon cardamom

1. Line an 8–inch pan with foil, smoothing.
2. Chop unsweetened chocolate and place in medium bowl with chocolate chips, Ricemellow Creme, and extracts.
3. Boil the sugar, almond milk, margarine, and cardamom until it reaches 234° F.
4. Pour boiling milk mixture onto chocolate, mixing quickly until all is combined well. Just as it is losing its gloss and thickening (about to set) pour into pan.
6. Smooth top with spatula. Chill. After a few minutes, before it sets completely, cut into squares. Store in covered container in the fridge.

Butterscotch Fudge

YIELD: AN 8–INCH PAN

Exceptionally smooth and very cheap to make — you'll never spend $10 a pound on fudge again!

Thermometer

3 cups sugar
1 cup soymilk
dash of salt
5 tablespoons margarine
3 teaspoons vanilla

1. Use a large pot. Grease an 8–inch pan.
2. Combine sugar, soymilk, and salt in a large pot over medium heat. Stir continually until the sugar dissolves and the mixture boils.
3. Turn down the heat a little and cook until candy reaches 238° F — soft ball stage (drop a little fudge into glass of cold water. It should form a ball and when you take the ball out it should flatten between your fingers.) Do not stir while it is boiling!
4. Take pot off the heat and add margarine. Let cool to 110° F. Add vanilla and beat vigorously. Keep beating until the fudge thickens and starts to lose its gloss. This means it's nearly set, so quickly pour into your small greased pan.
5. Chill and store in covered container in the fridge.

Chocolate Fudge

YIELD: AN 8–INCH PAN

This fudge is richer than the fudge in my previous book,
Lickin' the Beaters: Low Fat Vegan Desserts.

Pastry brush
Thermometer

1 cup soymilk
3 ounces unsweetened chocolate
2½ cups sugar
3 tablespoons agave or corn syrup
¼ cup margarine
1½ teaspoons vanilla

1. Grease an 8–inch pan. On medium heat, melt the soymilk and chocolate together in a large pot. Stir in the sugar and syrup. Cook the candy until it reaches 236° F, without stirring.
2. When sugar crystals form on sides of pot wipe with wet pastry brush. When candy reaches desired temperature take off heat. Add margarine, without stirring. Let stand until 110° F.
3. Add the vanilla and beat until it begins to lose its gloss. Pour into pan and chill in fridge.

Chocolate Banana Fudge

YIELD: ABOUT A POUND

Pastry brush
Thermometer

2 ounces unsweetened chocolate, chopped
1 cup white sugar
¾ cup soymilk
½ cup brown sugar
1 small, ripe banana, mashed (about ⅓ cup)
2 tablespoon Just Like Honey or corn syrup
dash of salt
3 tablespoon margarine
¼ cup ground almond
¼ cup finely shredded coconut, toasted (optional)
1 teaspoon vanilla

1. Grease a loaf pan. Heat the chocolate, sugars, soymilk, banana, honey/syrup, and salt in a large pot. Stir until sugar dissolves then cook over medium heat until candy reaches 236° F. Wash down sugar crystals on side of pot with wet brush.
2. Remove from heat, add margarine, and cool to 110° F. Add the almond, coconut (if using), and vanilla. Beat until it thickens and pour into pan.
3. Cool and cut into pieces when firm.

Penuche (Brown Sugar Fudge)

YIELD: ABOUT ONE POUND (12 GOOD-SIZED PIECES)

This is a creamy, caramel-flavored fudge.

Pasty brush
Thermometer

2¼ cup light brown sugar
¾ cup soymilk
pinch of salt
3 tablespoons margarine
1 teaspoon vanilla
1 cup roughly chopped walnuts

1. In a large pot bring the sugar, soymilk, and salt to a boil, mixing until all the sugar is dissolved. Cook until syrup reaches 238° F; do not stir. Wipe down the sugar crystals with a damp brush a few times while cooking.
2. Place wax paper, parchment paper, or lightly greased foil into a loaf pan, reaching up halfway to the sides.
2. Take pot off heat and add the margarine; don't stir. Let cool to 110° F. Add the vanilla and nuts and beat until it loses its gloss and is about to set. Pat into pan. Chill.

I am not one for putting nuts into fudge, but Penuche is different. It wouldn't be quite the same without them.

Date Nut Fudge

YIELD: ABOUT ONE POUND

Pastry brush
Thermometer

2 cups sugar
½ cup soymilk
3 tablespoons ground almonds
1 tablespoon agave syrup
2 tablespoons margarine
1 cup chopped dates
1½ teaspoon vanilla
½ cup chopped walnuts

1. Grease an 8–inch pan. In a large pot mix the sugar, soymilk, almonds, and agave and cook on medium. Stir to dissolve the sugar and then afterwards only occasionally. Cook until syrup reaches 236° F, washing down sugar crystals on the sides of the pot with a damp pastry brush.
2. Remove from heat and add margarine. Let cool until 110° F. Add dates and vanilla, beating well. Pour into a pan. It will cover about ¾ of the pan. Sprinkle nuts and press down firmly.

Caramelized Popcorn

YIELD: 3½ QUARTS

This candy is not fully coated like regular caramel corn and is a nice mixture of sweet and salty.

Thermometer

1 cup brown sugar
⅓ cup corn syrup
⅓ cup water
¼ teaspoon salt
1½ tablespoons margarine
½ teaspoon baking soda
½ teaspoon vanilla
3.5 quarts (14 cups) popped popcorn (remove unpopped kernels)

1. I suggest popping your corn on the stovetop. It tastes so much better than air-popped and it's easy! Coat the bottom of a pot with oil and put one layer of kernels at the bottom. Heat over medium high, shaking every once in while. When you start to hear the kernels pop, shake more. When the popping starts to die down, take off heat. Using a large soup pot will get you enough popcorn for this recipe.
2. Mix sugar, corn syrup, and water in a medium size pan. Cook at medium heat, stirring frequently.
3. When the mixture reaches 290° F, take off heat and stir in the salt. You may find that the temperature lurches up when you put the salt in. In that case, wait a few seconds before putting back on the stovetop. Continue to boil until the mixture reaches 300° F.
4. Remove from heat and add margarine, baking soda, and vanilla. Stir well. Slowly pour over popcorn, doing your best to coat all the kernels.
5. Spread out on a clean surface and let cool. Break into pieces.

Store in airtight container in the freezer and you'll have a convenient sweet that will last for months… or serve at a party and it will be gone in minutes.

Caramel Corn

YIELD: ABOUT 9 CUPS

Much richer than the Caramelized Popcorn, this recipe is from Deb Stoiber, who takes care of old movies. I guess spontaneously combustible film and candy making do go hand-in-hand!

¾ cup packed brown sugar
6 tablespoons margarine
3 tablespoons corn syrup
¼ teaspoon vanilla
¼ teaspoon baking soda
8 cups popped popcorn (unpopped kernels removed)

1. Preheat oven to 300° F. Pour popcorn into a large baking pan (3.5 quarts).
2. In medium pot mix brown sugar, margarine, and corn syrup. Stir and cook over medium heat until mixture boils. Without stirring, continue boiling at moderate and steady rate.
3. Remove pot from heat, stir in vanilla and baking soda. Pour caramel mixture over popcorn and stir gently to coat.
4. Bake in oven for 15 minutes. Stir, then return to oven and bake another 5 minutes. Remove from oven.
5. Spread caramel corn on foil or greased baking sheet to cool.

Light Toffee Popcorn

Thermometer

6 cups popcorn, unpopped kernels removed
1 cup mixed almonds and pecans, toasted
1⅓ cup sugar
½ cup margarine
½ cup corn syrup
1 teaspoon vanilla

1. Preheat oven to 200° F.
2. Mix the popcorn and nuts, place on baking sheet in oven to warm.
2. In a large pot mix the sugar, margarine, and corn syrup. Boil and simmer until 275° F.
3. Pour the popcorn and nuts into a large bowl. Add the vanilla to the syrup and mix well.
4. Coat the popcorn with the syrup and place on baking sheet. Separate the best you can with a wooden spoon. Cool and then break into pieces. Store in airtight container.

Popcorn Balls — Halloween Style

YIELD: ABOUT 18 BALLS

There's nothing quite like those popcorn balls you'd get in your loot bag at Halloween. If you were lucky and your parents didn't think there were razor blades in them, you'd get a great stick–to–your–teeth treat.

Thermometer

½ cup sugar
¼ cup plus 2 tablespoons water
2 tablespoons corn syrup
¼ teaspoon vinegar
pinch of salt
¼ teaspoon vanilla
7 cups popcorn (unpopped kernels removed)
oil

1. In a large pot combine sugar, water, salt, corn syrup, and vinegar. Heat until candy reaches 250° F.
2. Remove from heat and stir in vanilla. In a large bowl pour candy over popcorn, stir lightly to mix.
3. Oil your hands and form the popcorn into balls. Wrap in plastic wrap.

Krack That Jack!

YIELD: ABOUT 6 CUPS

A homemade vegan version of the candy you like to eat at the anarchist ballpark!
Hide small plastic toys in your bag of candy for that old fashioned effect.

Thermometer

5 cups popped corn (unpopped kernels removed)
⅔ cup Spanish peanuts
¼ cup fancy molasses
¼ cup maple syrup
¼ cup sugar

1. Mix popcorn and peanuts together in a large pot.
2. Cook the molasses, maple syrup, and sugar until it reaches 235° F.
3. Pour over popcorn to coat evenly. Break into pieces when fully cooled. Store in an airtight container.

Old-Fashioned Maple Sugar Candy

YIELD: ONE POUND

The queen of candy, it dates back more than 200 years.
Simple, elegant, super sweet and mapley.

Thermometer

2 cups maple syrup

1. In a large pot bring the maple syrup to a boil. Turn on low heat and simmer until it is 233° F.
2. Cool until 110° F. Then beat with wooden spoon until it turns light colored and creamy.
3. Pour into greased molds or form patties on wax paper. Cool.

Caramel Apples

YIELD: 14–15 SMALL APPLES

When was the last time you had one of these? Another great kitchen combo.

Wooden skewers
Thermometer

14–15 small apples
4 tablespoons margarine
2 cups brown sugar
1 cup light corn syrup
dash of salt
¾ cup soy yogurt
1 cup soymilk
½ teaspoon vanilla
1½ cups chopped peanuts (or other nuts)

1. Wash apples and pat dry. Remove stems and insert wooden skewer.
2. In a large pot melt margarine and stir in sugar, corn syrup, and salt. Bring to a boil over medium heat, stirring constantly. Add the soy yogurt and soymilk, mixing well.
3. Heat to 245° F, stirring constantly. Remove from heat and add vanilla.
4. Dip each apple into caramel, coating well. Dip bottoms into nuts. Set onto a well oiled baking sheet or wax paper and chill in fridge.
5. When chilled and set wrap in plastic and store in fridge.

Deluxe Caramel Apples

YIELD: 6 LARGE APPLES

Extremely decadent desserts are all the rage now, and you've probably seen these deluxe caramel apples in the window of confectionaries.

Wooden skewers
Thermometer

6 large apples

Choose your caramel:
Caramel Apple recipe (page 30)
or Soft Caramel (page 39)
or Strawberry Caramel (page 40)
or Honee Banana Caramel (page 41 — double the recipe)
1 cup minced walnuts / pecans / cashews
½ cup melted chocolate

1. Follow the Caramel Apple recipe (page 30) with your caramel of choice.
2. Once you've bathed the apple in caramel, freeze for a few minutes so the candy doesn't slide off.
3. Roll in nuts and add melted chocolate. Freeze for a few minutes more and serve.

You can add whatever your heart's desire after the caramel — fondant (page 48 or 50), candied ginger, candied nuts, crushed cookies, chopped fudge, minced chocolate bars, etc. Eat on a plate, cut up, not off the skewers!

Maple Syrup Butterscotch

YIELD: 8–INCH PAN

Pastry brush
Thermometer

1 cup sugar
½ cup water
¾ cup maple syrup
⅓ cup good-quality margarine
dash of salt

1. Grease an 8–inch pan. Mix all ingredients in a medium pot on low heat, stirring until sugar dissolves.
2. Boil until 300° F, do not stir. Wipe off any sugar crystals that form on sides of pot with a pastry brush — this will prevent grainy candy.
3. When candy reaches 300° F pour into pan. Do *not* scrape out every last bit in the pot.
4. Let cool at room temperature for a few minutes and then mark into squares before it sets up completely.

A really simple candy recipe, but easily turns grainy, so watch out for those sugar crystals. Make sure you use tasty margarine since the flavor really comes through.

Mava Burfi

YIELD: ABOUT A POUND OF CANDY

Burfi is delectable East Indian fudge often flavored with ground nuts, cardamom and rosewater. Khoya is a cheese-like substance traditionally made from cooking down milk. Finding vegan Indian sweets is pretty much impossible so you may end up making this concoction over and over, as it is highly addictive.

Khoya (makes about 2 cups):
8 cups soymilk (a kind you like to drink)
½ cup soymilk powder
¼ cup coconut oil
5 tablespoons lemon juice

1. Whisk the soymilk and soymilk powder in a heavy large-bottom pot. Heat on medium until boiling. Stir frequently.
2. Stir in the lemon juice and simmer on high. Keep stirring to keep the mixture from sticking, burning, or boiling over. Simmer until most of the liquid is gone — it will be about the consistency of cottage cheese or a very thick lumpy pudding. This will take about an hour.

Burfi:
2 cups khoya
1½ cups icing sugar
2 teaspoons cardamom
about 4 sheets of edible silver foil (optional)

1. Mix the khoya with the icing sugar and cardamom in a heavy bottomed pot. Cook on low, stirring continuously.
2. When the mixture comes together into a soft ball, looking like cookie dough, it is finished. It will take about 10 or 15 minutes. Don't rush, or you might burn your candy or take it off before it dries out enough.
3. Place on large board. Flatten with hands or rolling pin to about ½ inch thickness. Place optional silver foil on top. When cool, store in an airtight container in fridge. Eat when chilled and firm!

I highly recommend using a non–stick pan for both khoya and mava burfi. Usually I insist on non–toxic stainless steel but all the cooking down leaves soy caked in rings on your pans. It is really hard to take off when it happens. Silver foil can be found in East Indian grocery stores and online.

Buttery Chocolate Walnut Crunch

YIELD: ABOUT A POUND

This is melt-in-your-mouth good.

Thermometer

1 cup sugar
½ cup margarine
¼ cup water
¼ teaspoon salt
1 cup chopped walnuts
1 cup chocolate chips

1. Oil a baking sheet. Melt sugar, margarine, water, and salt and heat until it reaches 270° F (soft crack). Stir continually, but gently.
2. Add half the walnuts and stir well to incorporate sugar and margarine.
3. Pour onto baking sheet and spread to ¼ inch thick. Cool.
4. Melt chocolate chips in double boiler (or smaller pot on top of larger pot of simmering water.)
5. Spread on cooled candy. Sprinkle the rest of the nuts and press into chocolate. Chill in fridge and break into pieces.

Portland Peanut Butter Truffles

YIELD: ABOUT 20 PIECES

*When I fretted about a dish I had made for a Portland dessert potluck
I whipped up a batch of these in 20 minutes as backup.*

1 cup chocolate chips
¼ cup natural peanut butter
1 tablespoon icing sugar
⅛ teaspoon salt
1 tablespoon soy cream or soymilk
2 tablespoons finely chopped walnuts

1. On low heat melt all except soy cream and walnuts in a small pot. Make sure there are no lumps.
2. When it's melted and smooth pour in the soy cream and stir quickly! Basically you are purposely seizing the chocolate so you have to stir out any lumps very quickly. The chocolate will form a ball, like dough.
3. Pour into bowl and chill let sit a few minutes to cool to lukewarm.
4. Spread walnuts on baking sheet or plate. Break off bite-sized pieces of chocolate, roll into ball using your hands and roll into walnuts.
5. Place in airtight container. The truffles will be fresh for about a week — you can refrigerate them to increase their lifespan.

Chocolate Almond Dates

YIELD: ABOUT 24

Easy peasy and incredibly yummy — a recipe for those who want a healthier sweet.

½ cup chocolate chips
22–25 pitted whole dates (honey dates are good — no, there's no honey in them!)
22–25 raw almonds

1. Place wax paper on baking sheet. Melt chips on a double boiler (or a smaller pot on top of a bigger pot of simmering water.)
2. Stuff the almonds into the dates. Dip one end of each date into the chocolate.
3. Place on baking sheet and chill.

Frosted Pecans

YIELD: ABOUT 4 CUPS

Lightly sweet and creamy.

Thermometer

3½ cups pecan halves
1 cup sugar
½ cup tofu sour cream
2 teaspoon vanilla

1. Lightly oil 2 baking sheets.
2. Combine the sugar, tofu sour cream, and vanilla in a large pot and mix over medium–low heat. Stir frequently until it reaches 234° F. Remove from heat and mix in the pecans.
3. Turn out onto baking sheets. Separate nuts with 2 forks. Let stand at room temperature until set.

Creamy Cinnamon Walnuts

YIELD: ABOUT 3 CUPS

My friend Michele says these taste like a certain chain-store pastry…
I agree — except these nuts are better because they don't get weird and gross the next day!

1 cup sugar
½ cup tofu sour cream
2 tablespoons margarine
⅛ teaspoon salt
1 teaspoon vanilla
1 teaspoon cinnamon
2 cups walnut halves

1. Lightly oil 2 baking sheets.
2. Heat the sugar, tofu sour cream, margarine, and salt in a large pot on medium heat. Stir until sugar is dissolved and then heat until 236° F. Take off heat and let stand 15 minutes.
3. Add the vanilla and cinnamon and stir until mixture starts to lose its gloss. Toss in the nuts and coat well. Pour nuts onto baking sheets and separate with forks or leave connected. Cool and break apart if needed.

Pumpkin Walnuts

YIELD: ABOUT 3 CUPS

Thermometer

2 cups sugar
¼ cup tofu sour cream
¼ cup canned pumpkin
2 tablespoons margarine
⅛ teaspoon salt
1 teaspoon vanilla
½ teaspoon cinnamon
¼ teaspoon nutmeg
⅛ teaspoon cloves
⅛ teaspoon ginger
2¼ cups pecan halves

1. Lightly oil 2 baking sheets.
2. Heat the sugar, tofu sour cream, pumpkin, margarine, and salt in a large pot on medium heat. Stir until sugar is dissolved and then cook until candy reaches 236° F. Take off heat and let stand 15 minutes.
3. Add the vanilla and spices and stir until mixture starts to get thick. Move onto the next step just before it starts to lose its gloss.
4. Quickly now: toss in the nuts and coat well. Pour nuts onto sheets and separate with forks or leave connected. Cool and break apart if needed.

Hedgehog Chocolates

YIELD: 22 PIECES

Harsh-looking on the outside, yet surprisingly fresh on the inside.

2 cups chocolate chips
2 teaspoons lime juice
1 tablespoon margarine
pinch of ginger

1. In a small pot on low heat, melt together 1½ cups of the chocolate chips with the lime juice and margarine.
2. When cool enough to handle form into 22 small balls and place on baking sheet. Chill.
3. In a small pot on low heat melt the remaining ½ cup of chocolate chips and then add the ginger.
4. With two forks, roll the chilled balls into the pot of ginger chocolate, leaving the little spikies that form from the forks.
5. Place on baking sheet to chill in fridge until set.

Cluster Bomb Units

YIELD: ABOUT 10 MEDIUM SIZE PIECES

The best anti-war punk bands have great names for candy.
(Cluster Bombs are horrible little devices that litter little bomblets everywhere. Most do not
explode immediately, which means civilians are apt to be maimed or killed by them.
They also unfortunately look very much like toys. Evil, evil, evil!)

1½ cups chocolate chips
1 tablespoon margarine
1½ cups pecans, chopped
2 tablespoons brown sugar

1. Melt chocolate in a double boiler.
2. Melt the margarine in a frying pan and add chopped pecans and sugar. Fry for a few minutes — don't burn!
3. Mix the nuts and chocolate. Chill in freezer for a few minutes to cool slightly.
4. Spoon tablespoons of the mix onto a baking sheet covered with tinfoil. Place fridge and chill until firm.

Soft Caramel

YIELD: 8–INCH PAN

Pastry brush
Thermometer

1¾ cups soymilk
¼ cup oil
2 cup sugar
1 cup corn syrup
⅓ cup margarine
pinch of salt
2 teaspoon vanilla

1. Lightly grease an 8 x 8–inch pan. Blend ¾ cup of the soymilk with the oil.
2. Combine the rest of the ingredients in a large pot, including the last cup of soymilk, but set aside the vanilla. Cook mixture on medium heat. Stir until sugar is dissolved and mixture is brought to a boil. Stop stirring! Lower heat to a low simmer and continue cooking until candy reaches 240° F. Use a wet pastry brush to wash down the sugar crystals that form on the sides. These crystals will cause your candy to become gritty.
3. At 240° F stir constantly to avoid burning until mixture reaches 248° F. Remove from heat and add the vanilla.
4. Stir well and pour into pan. Do not scrape out the pot — this is another way to get gritty candy.
5. Cover with plastic wrap and chill.

Leftover caramel can be used in candy bars, Chocolate Tortoises (page 42), Chocolate Pebbles (page 42), or Tiger Eyes (page 61).

Strawberry Caramel

YIELD: ABOUT 3 CUPS

If you are lucky enough to live in Canada you can use strawberry soymilk to bring out the flavor.

Thermometer
Pastry brush

2 cups sugar
⅔ cup soymilk
½ container Suzanne's Strawberry Ricemellow Creme (5 ounces)
¼ cup margarine
½ teaspoon vanilla

1. Line a loaf pan with foil. Grease foil.
2. Heat the sugar and soymilk in a large pot on medium so it is a rolling boil, don't stir after sugar has dissolved. Stir in the Ricemellow.
3. Wash down sugar crystals with wet pastry brush.
4. When mixture reaches 234° F take off heat and add margarine and vanilla on top.
5. Beat well and pour into pan and chill.

Honee Banana Caramel

YIELD: ABOUT 2 CUPS

This is a soft caramel you can use to coat apples (page 31) or make Chocolate Pebbles (page 42.)

Pastry brush
Thermometer

1 cup sugar
1 cup brown sugar
3 ripe bananas (about 1 cup), mashed
¾ cup soymilk
¼ cup Just Like Honey
dash of salt
¼ cup margarine
1 teaspoon vanilla

1. Grease a loaf pan. Cook sugars, bananas, soymilk, Just Like Honey, and salt. Stir until sugar dissolves and then cook over medium heat until candy reaches 230° F. Stir only to prevent sticking on the bottom. Wash down sugar crystals on side of pot with wet pastry brush.
2. Remove from heat and add margarine. Cool to 110° F. Add vanilla and beat with wooden spoon until it thickens. Pour into pan.

Chocolate Tortoises

YIELD: 12 PIECES

This one is super easy if you have your caramel made already.

¾ cup chocolate chips
36 pecan halves
¼ cup Soft Caramel (page 39)

1. Melt the chocolate in a double boiler (or smaller pot on top of a larger pot of simmering water.)
2. Lightly grease a baking sheet and lay out 3 pecan halves (in a triangle) per tortoise in rows.
3. Spoon one teaspoon of caramel on top of each Tortoise. If soft enough, flatten the caramel out on top of the nuts.
4. Spoon the melted chocolate over the caramel nuts. Use a generous amount, but leave the ends of the pecans showing. Chill in fridge and when firm remove carefully from pan. Store in airtight container in fridge, separating the rows of Tortoises with wax paper.

Chocolate Pebbles

YIELD: 1 CUP OF CANDY PIECES

This is a good recipe for leftover caramel and chocolate.

½ cup chocolate chips
½ cup chilled Soft Caramel (page 39)

1. Melt the chocolate chips in a double boiler (or a smaller pot on top of a larger pot of simmering water.) Lightly grease a baking sheet.
2. Roll the caramel into small balls, about the size of the tip of your pinky finger.
3. Working quickly, cover the caramel balls in chocolate. You can put them directly in the melted chocolate pot and move them around with a spoon. Take them out of the chocolate and place on baking sheet. The caramel will melt and flatten — the candies will resemble pebbles.
4. Chill and then carefully remove and store in an airtight container in the fridge.

You can vary the size of the caramel balls to get various-sized candy.

Cinnamon Nuts

YIELD: ABOUT 3½ CUPS

QUICK RECIPE

This one is as easy as it gets. It doesn't take long to reach the desired temperature.

Thermometer

3 cups raw almonds or pecans (or use roasted unsalted nuts)
1 cup sugar
6 tablespoons soymilk
2 teaspoons cinnamon
½ teaspoon vanilla

1. Dry roast the raw nuts on baking sheet at 350° F for about 10 minutes.
2. Mix the sugar, soymilk, and cinnamon and boil at medium high, stirring constantly, until it reaches 236° F.
3. Add nuts to the sugar mixture. Add vanilla quickly and beat until creamy. Turn out onto wax paper and separate nuts with two forks.

Almond Toffee

YIELD: ABOUT A POUND

Pastry brush
Thermometer

1 cup good-quality margarine
1½ cups packed brown sugar
¾ cup chopped almonds

1. In a medium pot melt margarine over low heat and then add the sugar and almonds.
2. Stir slowly and continually over medium heat for 5 minutes until a light brown color. With a wet pastry brush, wash down the sugar crystals that form on the sides of the pot. (You're aiming for 300° F. The mixture will start dark brown and then bubble into a tan color. That's your cue it's ready to take off the heat.)
3. Pour thinly onto ungreased 9 x 13–inch pan. Score into bite-size pieces while still warm and not completely set.
4. Break into pieces when cool.

*For **Score! Bars**, that are perfect to bring your hot vegan date, melt 2 cups of chocolate and dip the cooled pieces of toffee to coat. Set on wax paper to firm.*

Salt Water Taffy

YIELD: ABOUT 50 PIECES

I suggest doing half a recipe to start with, as there are many steps involved, especially if you are doing multiple flavors. Good flavors are berry, lemon, banana, and cinnamon.

Wax paper
Scissors
Thermometer

2 cups sugar
2 tablespoons cornstarch
1 cup corn syrup
¾ cup water
2 tablespoons margarine
¾ teaspoon salt
½ teaspoon oil based flavoring or 1½ teaspoons regular flavoring extract

1. Cut out 50 small rectangles of wax paper (about 3x4 inches) and grease a baking sheet or marble slab.
2. Mix the sugar and cornstarch in a large pot. Stir out any lumps. Add the corn syrup, water, margarine, and salt. Heat on medium until sugar dissolves.
3. Cover pot and boil for 2 minutes. Uncover and cook until temperature reaches 266° F. At this temperature a drop of syrup will make a hard, yet squeezable ball in cold water.
4. Remove from heat and add flavor. If you are making different flavors from the same batch evenly distribute the flavor extracts in several different mugs large enough to hold a wooden spoon. Gently stir the syrup and flavor together.
5. Pour out onto greased surface. Keep watch over your taffy. As soon as it is cool enough to touch begin pulling it with greased hands. It will become light and take on a satin gloss.
6. Pull into a thin rope (1½ inches wide) and place on a piece of wax paper. Using scissors cut "rope" into bite-size pieces and wrap in wax paper, twisting the ends. Store in an airtight container at room temperature.

Maple Nut Chocolates

YIELD: 24 SMALL PIECES

Wax paper

1⅓ cups toasted finely chopped nuts
½ cup icing sugar, sifted
¼ cup maple syrup
¼ teaspoon natural maple flavoring (optional)
½ cup chocolate chips

1. Mix 1 cup of the nuts with the icing sugar, maple syrup, and flavoring. Form 24 small balls.
2. Roll the balls in the remaining nuts. Chill on plate or baking sheet.
3. Melt the chocolate on a double boiler (or a smaller pot on top of a larger pot of simmering water.)
4. Remove the chocolate from the heat and dip the maple balls into chocolate. Set onto wax paper and chill in fridge.

Honee Roasted Peanuts

¼ cup Just Like Honey
¼ cup brown sugar
2 tablespoons margarine
¼ teaspoon salt
2 cups salted peanuts

1. Preheat oven to 350° F.
2. In a medium pot melt Just Like Honey, sugar, margarine, and salt and simmer a minute or so on medium heat.
3. Mix the syrup with the nuts. Roast nuts until golden — 6 to 9 minutes. Watch carefully to prevent burning or over-roasting.

Candied Mint Leaves

YIELD: 25 PIECES

3 tablespoon sugar
¼ teaspoon peppermint extract
1 teaspoon arrowroot mixed with 2 teaspoon water
25 mint leaves, stems removed

1. Mix the sugar with the peppermint extract and put in sifter.
2. Dip your finger into the mixed arrowroot and water and rub onto both sides of each mint leaf. Place on plate.
3. Sift the sugar on one side of the mint leaves, turn over and sugar the other side. Leaves need to be wet in order to get the sugar to stick so re–wet any dried-out leaves with arrowroot mixture.
4. Place mint leaves close together on cooking rack and leave in a warm place to dry. This can take up to 2 or 3 days so you might want to double the recipe.

Creamy Fondant

YIELD: 60–70 PIECES

It's this kind of recipe that makes you feel like a Candy Queen.
When you've got your scraper going and your liquid eventually becomes so many different
wonderful centers for chocolates, you feel like you're totally invincible.

Slab of marble and metal bars for making candy
OR large baking sheet with sides, plus wire cooling rack
Pastry brush
Thermometer
3–5–inch metal scraper
Dampened kitchen towel

2½ cups sugar
1 cup soymilk
3 tablespoons margarine, cut up
¼ teaspoon cream of tartar

Optional:
½ teaspoon of oil-based flavoring and/or
½ cup finely chopped nuts and/or
½ cup coconut

1. If using the marble and metal bars make a 12 x 18–inch area on the marble. Or place the baking sheet on top of the cooking rack. Place a cup of hot water containing pastry brush and thermometer next to cooking area.

2. Mix all the ingredients in a very large pot. Cook on medium heat, stirring constantly until sugar is dissolved and mixture is nearly boiling. Wash the sugar crystals down the sides of the pot with a wet pastry brush, clip thermometer into pot, and cook until temperature reaches 236° F (it will about 15 minutes.) Stop stirring. Wash the sides of the pot a few more times before reaching desired temperature.

3. Once the candy reaches 236° F take off heat and immediately pour onto marble surface or baking sheet. Cool until medium warm, about 15 minutes. It will be ready when you put your finger on the edge of the candy and the indentation stays. Keep finger checking to a minimum as fondant doesn't like to be handled at this stage.

4. Using your scraper, take an edge of the candy and move it towards the middle. Do this to all sides and keep at it, moving the candy constantly. It will be like liquid to start, but will begin to firm up after about 5 minutes. It will lose its gloss and get firmer and firmer. The candy is ready when it starts to become dry and the scraper can stand up straight in the fondant.

5. Knead fondant with your hands into a smooth ball, wrap in a damp kitchen towel and place in an airtight container. Chill in fridge.

6. To form centers for dipping remove from fridge and let warm to room temperature. Flour a surface. Add oil-based flavoring if desired. Knead flavorings in on floured surface. Cover and return to fridge until chilled. Form into balls when ready to dip in chocolate.

Traditional Fondant

Slab of marble and metal bars for making candy
OR large baking sheet with sides and wire cooling rack
Pastry brush
Thermometer
3–5–inch metal scraper
Wax paper

3 cups sugar
1 cup hot water
¼ teaspoon cream of tartar
flavoring (optional)

1. If using the marble and metal bars, make a 12 x 18–inch area on the marble. Or place the baking sheet on top of the cooking rack. Place a cup of hot water containing pastry brush and thermometer next to cooking area.

2. If using an electric stove turn the burner on high. Mix the sugar and hot water together in a large pot and place on the hot burner. Stir in the cream of tartar and continue stirring constantly until sugar has melted. Boil on high heat until it reaches 240° F. Stop stirring. Wash the sugar crystals down the sides of the pot with the wet pastry brush 2 or 3 times. This process will take about 10 minutes.

3. At 240° F immediately remove from heat and pour onto marble or baking sheet. Cool until medium warm, about 30 minutes. The candy will be ready when you put your finger on the edge and the indentation stays. Keep finger checking to a minimum as fondant doesn't like to be handled at this stage.

4. Use your scraper and take an edge of the candy and move it towards the middle. Do this to all sides and keep at it, moving the candy constantly. It will be liquid to start, and then start to firm up after 5 minutes. The candy will lose its gloss and get firmer and firmer. It is ready when it starts to become dry and the scraper can stand up straight in the fondant.

5. Knead with your hands into a smooth ball. Use immediately or wrap with a damp kitchen towel and store in an airtight container. It will keep at room temperature for a few days or in the fridge for a few months.

6. When ready to use candy dust a large piece of wax paper with flour. Form fondant into balls. Let sit at room temperature for 30 minutes to crust over.

To make flavored fondant add 1 tsp of any flavoring at the end of the kneading process
(step 5). You can also add it after it's been in the fridge — just bring to room temperature first.
To make dipped chocolates more exciting you can use fondant to cover them or any center.
Melt the fondant to a thin consistency to dip. Any melted fondant can be used for more dipping,
but not as centers.

Peppermint Patties

YIELD: 20 PIECES

1 batch Creamy Fondant (page 48), with ½ teaspoon peppermint flavor
2 cups chocolate chips
2 tablespoons margarine

1. Pat the fondant into 20 patties.
2. In a medium pot melt chocolate chips and margarine together on low heat.
2. Dip fondant patties into melted chocolate and dry on wax paper.

Cherry Cordial Chocolates

It seems that only people over the age of 50 actually like these confections,
but when you make them yourself they seem to taste really good! ;)

Kitchen towel
Thermometer
Wax Paper
Toothpick

1 can of Bing cherries
½ traditional fondant recipe (page 50)
1½ teaspoons cherry flavor
12 ounces chocolate chips (about 2 cups)

1. Drain the cherry juice (refrigerate and use in cakes, etc). Drain cherries on the kitchen towel for a few hours, as long as you can.

2. In a double boiler melt the fondant until it reaches 160° F. Dip the cherries into the fondant, coating well, and place on wax paper to harden, about 10 minutes. If the fondant gets too thick it will not cling to cherries. Place over hot water to melt more. If it is too thin it will not harden. Make sure there are no holes in the fondant! Repair with extra fondant and a toothpick. Make sure the fondant is not too hard or it will cause your hole to get bigger! Be careful when handling the cherries at this stage — the heat from your fingers can break the fondant.

3. You must dip the cherries in chocolate within the hour. Melt the chocolate in a double boiler and cool to about 88° F. Roll the fondant-coated cherries in the chocolate. Once again, make sure the entire cherry is fully coated in chocolate and fix holes. Don't worry about making them nice and round and pretty. This isn't the important part. Set on wax paper to dry.

4. After setting for an hour at room temperature, redip the bottoms of the cherries for more stability. Dip whole cherry again if they seem too delicate or have holes. DO NOT EAT IMMEDIATELY! Let the chocolates ripen at least 3 days.

Here is why this is the hardest recipe in this book and you must follow the directions properly: If the fondant has holes it will ooze cherry juice into your pot of chocolate and as you have read previously any liquid will RUIN your chocolate. Your whole pot of chocolate will have to be discarded (for another use) and you'll have to melt more. Also, if the fondant breaks inside the chocolate the cherry juice will just ooze out and will change the consistency of the candy. You want the juice and fondant to react with one another to become creamy. If there is a hole in the chocolate coating the candy will not last very long and the juice/fondant reaction will not work either. The dryer your cherries are the better luck you will have in this whole process. I suggest starting with about half of the cherries in the can for one sitting. I lost half of the cherries the first time I did this recipe. You need all your attention on these candies and no distractions!

Crafty Caramels

YIELD: ABOUT 50 PIECES

*Ooey-gooey caramels can be yours tomorrow if you rush right
into your kitchen and try this recipe today!*

Pastry brush
Thermometer

1½ cups corn syrup
1½ cups soymilk blended well with ½ cup oil
1⅓ cups sweetened condensed soymilk (page 129)
1 cup sugar
½ cup good-quality margarine
2 teaspoons vanilla flavor (oil or glycerin — not extract in alcohol)

1. Line an 8–inch pan with foil and grease. Mix all ingredients in a medium pot on medium heat. Stir constantly until sugar has melted. Lay — don't clip — the thermometer in pot. Wash down sides with wet pastry brush a few times during the cooking process. Stir frequently to prevent burning. Cook until mixture reaches 245° F, but also do the cold water test (see page 16) to get the firmness you desire.
2. As the cooking process reaches its end it will be necessary to stir more often to prevent sticking and burning. When it's reaches the firmness you like (use the cold water test) give the caramel a good few good stirs before pouring into your pan.
3. Allow to set and dry about 24 hours, room temperature. When you cut the caramels use a greased serrated knife and cut like a saw. Wrap in wax paper or plastic.

For Maple Caramels, replace the corn syrup with maple syrup and leave out the vanilla.

Crafty Chocolate Maple Caramels

YIELD: ABOUT 50 PIECES

Pastry brush
Thermometer

1 cup sugar
1 cup sweetened condensed soymilk (page 129)
¾ cup corn syrup
¾ cup maple syrup
⅓ cup margarine
2 ounces chopped unsweetened chocolate

1. Line an 8–inch pan with foil and grease. Mix everything but chocolate in a medium pot on medium heat. Stir constantly until sugar has melted. Lay — don't clip — the thermometer in pot. Wash down sides with wet pastry brush a few times during the cooking process. Stir frequently to prevent burning. Cook until mixture has reached 255° F, but also do the cold water test (page 16) to get the firmness you desire. Add the chocolate at 255° F.

2. As the cooking process reaches its end it will be necessary to stir more often to prevent sticking and burning. When it reaches the firmness you like (use the cold water test) give the caramel a good few good stirs before pouring into your pan.

3. Allow to set and dry about 24 hours at room temperature. When you cut the caramels, use a greased serrated knife and cut like a saw. Wrap in wax paper or plastic.

Nutmeg-Glazed Almonds

YIELD: ABOUT 2½ CUPS

Sweet and savory together. Looks nice too.

2 cups almonds
2 cups sugar
1 teaspoon nutmeg
1 teaspoon salt

1. Preheat oven to 300° F. When heated, place the almonds on a baking sheet and turn off heat.
2. Melt the sugar in a heavy bottomed skillet over medium high heat. A cast-iron one is good for this. Stir constantly until sugar is a golden brown syrup, about 10 minutes.
3. Remove from heat and quickly stir in nutmeg and salt. Pour quickly over warm nuts, coating evenly.
4. These nuts cool into a dark brown massive lollipop sheet with nuts. Break into pieces and store in an airtight container.

Pralines

YIELD: 12–15 PIECES

Pralines are like fudge with grain. They are easier to make because you don't have to be concerned with making them smooth.

Thermometer

2 cups pecan halves
3 cups brown sugar
⅓ cup soymilk blended with 3 tablespoon oil
pinch of salt
1 teaspoon vanilla

1. Preheat oven to 300° F. Place nuts in oven and turn off heat. Lay out wax paper for the candy.
2. Mix sugar, soymilk mixture, and salt in a large pot. Stir constantly over medium heat until sugar dissolves. Cook until mixture reaches 236° F, stirring frequently to keep from sticking.
3. Remove from heat and cool for 5 minutes. Add vanilla. Beat until it starts to thicken and add the pecans. Drop into rounds, 12–15, onto wax paper. If the candy starts to get too firm to allow nice smooth circles, add one or two drops of hot water to thin.

Chop this up, mix in with some vanilla soy ice creem, and you've got a luscious treat!

Chocolate Creem Cheeze Candy

YIELD: ABOUT 12 PIECES

This is kind of like a creem cheeze fudge but you wouldn't find me using the f–word for anything that doesn't boil to the "soft ball stage"!

½ tub vegan cream cheese (4 ounces)
2 cups icing sugar
3 ounces unsweetened chocolate, melted
½ teaspoon vanilla
pinch of salt

1. Grease a loaf pan. Beat the creem cheese with a fork. Gradually add the icing sugar, sifting into the bowl. Mix in the melted chocolate and stir in salt and vanilla.
2. Pour/pat into the loaf pan and chill until firm.

Add ½ teaspoon almond extract for Chocolate Almond Creem Cheeze Candy.

Peanut Butter Cups

YIELD: 12 PIECES

*These are the real thing! Those who shun the perfect combination
of chocolate and peanut butter cannot be of this world.*

Pastry brush
12 medium cupcake papers

1¼ cups chocolate chips
2½ tablespoons oil
2½ tablespoons soymilk powder
½ cup natural peanut butter
¼ cup icing sugar
¼ teaspoon salt

1. Cut the cupcake papers in half so they are half the original height. Melt the chocolate in a double boiler (or a smaller pot on top of a larger pot of simmering water) and gradually stir in the oil and soymilk powder. Mix well.
2. Paint the cups with the melted chocolate using your pastry brush. Paint a thin layer, but don't let the paper show through. About ¾ of a tablespoon of melted chocolate does the trick. Place the cups into a muffin tin. Chill in freezer until set.
3. Mix the peanut butter, salt, and sugar. Spread about 1 tablespoon into the set chocolate cups. Chill in freezer for 2 minutes.
4. Spread melted chocolate on top of the peanut butter and chill in fridge or freezer until set. Store in fridge and thaw at room temperature for a few minutes when ready to eat.

Walnut Figs

YIELD: 6 LARGE PIECES

I got this idea from attending a candy convention. Some Russian guys were selling these and told me they were dairy–free and healthy. I bought a box and noticed it was clearly marked with milk powder (and hydrogenated oil)! They pulled a fast one, so I'm stealing their idea and veganizing it!

1½ cups chocolate chips
3 tablespoons oil
3 tablespoons soymilk powder
6 walnut halves
6 dried figs, stems removed

1. Melt the chocolate in a double boiler (or a smaller pot on top of a larger pot of simmering water) with the oil and soymilk powder. Mix well.
2. Put a walnut on top of a fig and place on wax paper. Pour chocolate on top to cover. Let set.
3. Dip the bottoms of the figs into the chocolate. Cover thoroughly.
4. If there is some chocolate left, dip the figs another time.

Wonder–Full Chocolate Bars

YIELD: 16 BARS

In Canada and the UK there is a chocolate bar like this made by a famous company.
Now we have our own vegan version to drool over.

1 cup chocolate chips
2 tablespoons oil
2 tablespoons soymilk powder
1 cup natural peanut butter
3 tablespoons maple syrup
1 teaspoon salt
¼ cup + 1 tablespoon crisped rice cereal, lightly crushed
½ batch Soft Caramel (page 39)

1. Grease an 8–inch pan. Melt the chocolate chips in a double boiler (or a smaller pot on top of a larger pot of simmering water) and gradually stir in the oil and soymilk powder. Mix well.
2. Pour half pan and freeze until set. Mix the peanut butter with salt and maple syrup. Pat this onto the set chocolate.
3. Sprinkle the rice cereal on top of the peanut butter. Spread some caramel on top of that. Spread the remaining melted chocolate as the last layer.
4. Chill until set and let sit at room temperature a few moments before cutting and devouring.

For a less sweet chocolate bar, use less caramel.

Pumpkin Truffles

3 tablespoons cooked, mashed pumpkin
1 tablespoon soy yogurt
⅛ teaspoon nutmeg
½ teaspoon cinnamon
1 tablespoon plus 2 teaspoons sugar
1½ tablespoons margarine
6 ounces semisweet chocolate (1 cup)
2 tablespoons ground nuts

1. Mix the pumpkin, soy yogurt, nutmeg, ⅛ teaspoon of the cinnamon, and 2 teaspoons of sugar and margarine in a small pot. Heat on low for a few minutes until melted.
2. Melt chocolate in double boiler (or small pot on top of a larger pot of simmering water) and stir in pumpkin mixture.
3. Mix very well. Refrigerate in a bowl until firm.
4. Mix nuts with the remaining sugar and cinnamon. Scoop out rounded teaspoons of chocolate and roll into balls. Then roll into nuts. Store in airtight container in fridge.

QUICK RECIPE

Easy Chocolate Truffles

YIELD: ABOUT 30 MEDIUM SIZED PIECES

2 cups chocolate chips
2 tablespoons margarine
2 tablespoons soymilk
¼ cup ground nuts, fine coconut, cocoa, etc.

1. Melt the chocolate in a double boiler (a pot on top of a large pot of simmering water) and add the margarine and soymilk. When cool enough to handle, scoop out by the heaping teaspoons–full and roll into nuts, coconut, or cocoa.

Tiger Eyes

*These little bites were made for my friend Ben when he found
the Ohh David? Candy Bars (page 62) too sweet.*

*some Soft Caramel (page 39)
some minced salted peanuts
some chocolate chips*

1. When your caramel cools, scoop off little balls, roll in peanuts and stick a chocolate chip in the center.

Ohh David? Candy Bars

YIELD: 7 VERY LARGE BARS

*David Wilson always takes me into the Ranch and gives me work. I asked
"David Wilson — if you were a candy what would you be?" and he said
"Something with lavender" and I said "David Wilson, I don't think lavender and
chocolate go well together. Think of something chocolate" and he said
"I really like those chocolate bars with nougat and caramel and
peanuts" and I said "David Wilson, think of something else because no
vegan has ever made nougat at home." Surprise, surprise.*

Pastry brush
Thermometer
Electric mixer

Nougat:
3 cups sugar
⅔ cup hot water
¼ cup Just Like Honey or agave syrup
⅔ cup malt powder
2 tablespoons soymilk powder
2 teaspoons vanilla

1. Boil the sugar, water, and Just Like Honey in a very large pot. Stir constantly until sugar is dissolved and clip on thermometer .
2. When mixture reaches 230° F take out ⅔ cup and pour into a large mixing bowl. Sifted in soymilk powder and ⅓ cup malt powder and mix on high speed.
3. Continue cooking rest of mix, washing down sugar crystals at least twice more, until syrup reaches 265° F. This will take about 20 minutes.
4. Pour the syrup into the mixing bowl in a thin stream while mixer is on high. Sift in the rest of the malt powder and add vanilla. Mix until a stiff dough is formed.
5. Press into an 8 x 10–inch rectangle — either in a pan or wax paper — and chill.

If you want it less sweet and more barley tasting, replace 2 tablespoons of the Just like Honey with 2 tablespoons barley malt syrup.

1 recipe Soft Caramel (page 39)
3½ cup chocolate chips
1¼ cup finely chopped salted peanuts

1. Cut the nougat into 7 very large bars or many smaller ones. Let sit at room temperature.
2. Make the Soft Caramel and put in fridge. If you want to make your chocolate bars right away put caramel in freezer.
3. In a double boiler (or a smaller pot on top of a large pot of simmering water) melt the chocolate. Remove the caramel from fridge or freezer and coat one piece of nougat in the caramel.
4. Next coat the bar in peanuts and dip one side into melted chocolate.
5. Let sit on wax paper. Do one bar at a time, following the same pattern. When all bars have one side coated with chocolate put in freezer to set. Work quickly. You'll find the caramel easy to dip at the beginning and harder as you go on. If the caramel is too firm you can warm it on top of a pot on the double boiler. At the same time you'll see the caramel/peanut coating on your first bars begin to slide off. When this happens, squeeze to stabilize a round shape. If you work quickly, you can get a good number of your bars into the freezer before the caramel/peanuts start sliding off.
6. When one side of the dipped bar is set, coat the other side in melted chocolate. Return to freezer to chill. Once you've covered the bars in chocolate they will keep their shape. Your hands will get very sticky and candy-coated during this whole process.

Old Fashioned Maple Snow Candy

YIELD: 6 SERVINGS

Eat with a wooden spoon and wonder whether the pioneers would have done such awful things to Native Peoples if they had eaten more maple syrup.

Thermometer

2 cups maple syrup

1. Boil maple syrup on medium low. If it looks like it may boil over stir the surface.
2. When the syrup reaches 234° F, pour into bowls of clean snow.

Maple Taffy

YIELD: ONE POUND

Pastry brush
Thermometer

2 cups maple syrup
½ teaspoon baking powder
¼ cup margarine

1. Chill a baking sheet.
2. Boil everything until 260° F. Wipe down sugar crystals with wet pastry brush when they form on sides of the pan.
3. Put the baking sheet on top of a wire cake rack and pour the syrup onto the baking sheet.
4. When edges are cool enough to touch, fold into center. With greased hands, pull until satiny and glossy. Pull into a rope and then cut into pieces. Wrap in wax paper, twisting ends.

Candy becomes creamy after a few days.

Almond Snaps

QUICK RECIPE

YIELD: ABOUT A POUND

Who would think such a simple candy would be so heavenly?

Rolling pin

1 cup sugar
1 cup ground almonds

1. Grease a clean chopping board, a rolling pin, a knife and spatula. Put sugar into a large heavy bottomed skillet and cook on medium. Stir constantly until it is a golden brown liquid. Remove from heat and quickly add the nuts.
2. Pour onto board and roll very thin with rolling pin, about 6 x 17–inch. Cut into 2–inch pieces with knife. Use the spatula to loosen from board. As it cools make sure the pieces don't stick to the board or each other.

For Sesame Snaps replace ½ the sugar with ½ cup Just Like Honey and use sesame seeds instead of almonds.

Orange Walnuts

QUICK RECIPE

YIELD: ABOUT 4½ CUPS

A simple confection that will make even a health nut appreciate candy.

Thermometer

2 oranges
1½ cups sugar
½ teaspoon vanilla
pinch turmeric
3½ cups walnut halves

1. Put wax paper on two baking sheets. Finely grate 4 teaspoons of orange peel and squeeze one orange to get ¼ cup juice.
2. Boil the juice and sugar until it reaches 240° F. This won't take too long.
3. Add a little bit of turmeric for color and remove from heat. Add orange peel and vanilla and mix. Add the walnuts and mix well.
4. Stir until syrup begins to look cloudy and spread onto baking sheets. Separate with forks if you want.

Chocolate Pecan Cheeze Balls

YIELD: 22 PIECES

12 ounces chocolate chips (2 cups)
1 tub tofu cream cheese (8 ounces)
6 ounces mint candy (1 cup)
2 cups pecans

1. Blend the chocolate chips until crushed. Add to tofu cream cheese.
2. Blend the mint candy until crushed. Add to chocolate tofu cream cheese.
3. Mix these up well. Blend the pecans until crushed and mix into the rest.
4. Form 22 balls and keep chilled.

Crunch Chocolate Bars

YIELD: ABOUT HALF A POUND

*Created by Hannah, this is a popular honeycomb candy in Canada
and the UK that Americans have been known to cross the border for.
Do they realize there is a US version called Sea Foam that's sold by the ocean?
Look out for Hannah's* Southcoast Vegan Cooking Book. *southcoastvegan@hotmail.co.uk*

Thermometer

*1 cup sugar
1 cup corn syrup
1 tablespoon vinegar
1 tablespoon baking soda, sifted
1 cup chocolate chips*

1. Place aluminum foil in an 8 x 8–inch pan and grease the foil.
2. Place the sugar, corn syrup, and vinegar into a big heavy–bottom pot, heat gently until the sugar has completely dissolved.
3. Boil the mixture without stirring. Heat until 300° F. Remove from heat and mix in the baking soda, stirring quickly but thoroughly. You don't want to mix too much or too long or you'll lose a lot of the bubbling action.
4. Pour the candy quickly into your pan. Mixture will bubble into place. Allow to cool before breaking into chunks.
5. Melt the chocolate chips on a double boiler and then dip the candy into the melted chocolate and dry on a wire rack.

Coconut Mountain Bar

YIELD: ABOUT A POUND AND A HALF

Once again, Hannah impresses us all with her veganization of a popular chocolate bar. Write and ask her for her South Coast Cooking Zine: *southcoastvegan@hotmail.co.uk*

Wax or parchment paper

¾ cup margarine
⅓ cup soymilk
4 tablespoons icing sugar
1⅓ cups shredded coconut
1 teaspoon vanilla extract
1 cup chocolate chips

1. Grease and line an 8–inch pan with wax or parchment paper.
2. In a medium pot melt the margarine and add the soymilk and icing sugar, stirring thoroughly until it starts to boil. Remove from heat and add the coconut and vanilla.
3. Beat well with wooden spoon and pour into pan. Chill for an hour.
4. Melt the chocolate in a double boiler. Cut coconut into cubes and dip into chocolate. Dry on a wire rack.

Apricot Morsels

YIELD: ABOUT A POUND

3 tablespoons margarine
½ pound sifted icing sugar
1 tablespoon apple cider or orange juice
½ teaspoon vanilla
1 cup ground dried apricots (in food processor or blender)
fine coconut for rolling

1. In a medium pot melt the margarine and mix with sugar, juice, and vanilla.
2. Add the apricots to the mixture. Knead like dough.
3. Make dough into small balls and roll in coconut. Chill. Flavor improves with time.

Wacky Candy

YIELD: ABOUT 25 PIECES

Yep. Pretty much chocolate-covered croutons! Best not to tell your friends!

2 pieces of white bread
½ cup brown sugar
¼ cup margarine
2 tablespoons water
2 tablespoons ground nuts
1 cup chocolate chips
2 tablespoons margarine

1. Cut the bread into cubes, about 1 inch, to give you around 25 pieces. Let sit overnight.
2. In a large pot mix the brown sugar, margarine, and water together and boil for a couple minutes.
3. Add the nuts and mix well. Dredge the bread into the syrup and fry until golden brown. Let cool on wire rack.
4. In a large pot melt the chocolate with margarine on medium low heat. Coat the bread chunks in chocolate and dry on wire rack.

Cheddar Cheeze Candy

YIELD: ABOUT ONE POUND

Yes, that is correct.
This is an old-time candy that invites you to take a chance with your taste buds.

Electric mixer

1¼ *cups icing sugar*
1 *cup soy cheddar cheese (a kind that melts at least a little)*
½ *cup margarine*
½ *cup cocoa*
¾ *cup soymilk powder*
2 *teaspoons vanilla*
about 3 tablespoons soymilk

1. Grease a loaf pan. Mix all but the soymilk in a bowl with electric mixer. Add a bit of soymilk if you need to make the mixture creamy.
2. Pour into pan and chill until firm.

This recipe is better with powdered rice or soymilk in a carton, rather than soymilk powder in bulk (which is basically low fat soy flour). You may want to reduce the sugar if you use the packaged kind.

Oregon Apple Candy

YIELD: ABOUT ONE POUND

This is a fun candy to use fancy applesauce — apples with raspberries, mangos, blueberries, etc. make this one even more flavorful. If you use sweetened applesauce reduce sugar to 1⅓ cups.

2 cups sugar
1 tablespoon arrowroot starch
dash of salt
2 cups unsweetened applesauce
4 teaspoons agar powder
½ cup finely chopped walnuts
4 teaspoons lemon juice
1 teaspoon lemon peel
⅓ cup icing sugar

1. In a large pot mix the sugar, arrowroot starch, and salt. Mix in the applesauce. Sprinkle the agar on top. Let sit 10 minutes.
2. Cook the mixture for about half an hour on medium low, stirring frequently. It will become thick.
3. Mix in the walnuts, lemon juice, and lemon peel. Rinse an 8–10–inch glass dish with cold water and pour the apple mixture into it.
4. Let sit 24 hours on counter to dry. Remove from pan and cut into squares. Roll in icing sugar. Store in airtight container.

Apricot Log

YIELD: ABOUT 32 PIECES

½ cup minced dates
1 cup minced dried apricots
2 rounds dried pineapple, minced
½ cup ground animal crackers
¼ cup agave syrup
½ cup flaked coconut

1. Combine all the ingredients except the coconut. Mix well.
2. Place on wax paper and roll into a 16–inch log. Roll in coconut, pressing firmly.
3. Wrap in wax paper and chill. Cut into slices.

Summer Sausage Candy

YIELD: A 10–INCH ROLL

Thermometer

1 cup sugar
½ cup soymilk
1¼ cups chopped dates
1 cup flaked coconut
½ cup chopped walnuts

1. In a medium pot mix sugar and soymilk and cook until candy reaches 234° F. Stir every so often.
2. Add dates and cook a few minutes more, stirring constantly. Remove from heat and add the coconut and nuts.
3. Cool a little while then turn onto wax paper and shape into a 10–inch roll. Chill and slice.

Chocolate Leaves

YIELD: 15 PIECES

It's best not to even try this recipe on a warm day.

15 rose or mint leaves, with some stem
¼ cup chocolate chips

1. Wash and dry the rose leaves. Only use plants that haven't been treated with chemicals.
2. Melt chocolate in a double boiler and then let sit for about 10 minutes.
3. Coat one side of the dry leaves with chocolate using a small spatula or ideally a small clean paint brush. About ⅛–inch of chocolate works best. Chill in fridge for 5 minutes or until set.
4. Remove any chocolate that crept to the underside of the leaf then gently remove the leaf. You have a chocolate leaf!

Choco Almond Bites

YIELD: 20 PIECES

Simple. Nice.

½ cup ground almonds
½ cup cocoa
8 teaspoons Just Like Honey or agave syrup
dash of cinnamon (optional)
sugar to coat

1. Place ground almonds in a bowl and sift in cocoa. Mix.
2. Add the agave and mix well. Form in 20 small balls.
3. Roll in sugar.

For a "raw" dessert grind raw cacao nibs and use in place of cocoa. Use raw agave syrup.

Chocolate Haystacks

YIELD: 18 PIECES

1 cup chocolate chips
4 tablespoons margarine
2 cups large-shred coconut
½ cup quick-cooking oats
pinch of salt
2 tablespoons soymilk
½ teaspoon vanilla

1. In a small pot, sitting above simmer water, melt chocolate. Place the margarine on top to melt. Don't stir.
2. In a medium bowl mix the coconut, oats, and salt. Stir well.
3. Pour the chocolate/margarine into the dry, adding soymilk and vanilla.
4. Mix well and form into haystacks using a tablespoon — let sit to dry on wax paper.

Chocolate Garlic

YIELD: ABOUT 20 PIECES

This recipe comes from Joshua Ploeg, who travels around making food fit for royalty. He has written a collection of cookbooks with vegan recipes that will amaze, startle, and satisfy grumpy meat eaters. http://www.webspawner.com/users/joshuaplague/

2 heads garlic
oil to drizzle (nut oil recommended)
citrus juice to drizzle
sugar to sprinkle
1 cup chocolate chips
3 tablespoons margarine
2 teaspoons grated lime peel
pinch ground ginger

1. Preheat oven to 400° F. Semi-roast garlic on baking sheet by cutting the tops off, drizzling with oil, citrus juice and sugar. Roast for 15–25 minutes. If you are person who loves raw garlic, 15 minutes is fine. If raw garlic gives you the willies, go for the longer time. Allow to cool then peel off the skins. Sprinkle with juice and sugar if you wish.
2. Melt the chocolate with margarine and lime peel. Stir in the ginger.
3. Dip the cloves into the chocolate using skewers or toothpicks and coat them by twirling. Place on a baking sheet with wax paper and cool. Serve as a nice treat to some unsuspecting victim.

Chocolate Hints

Always melt chocolate in a double boiler — a pot of chopped chocolate sitting above a pot of hot water. Never ever let water get into your melting chocolate either by the bottom pot boiling too hard or moisture on your stirring spoon. If even one drop hits your melting chocolate it will seize up and will form hard globs and you'll have to start over.

You can also melt chocolate in the microwave — medium low temperature for 2 minutes, stirring every now and then.

An easy way to get a thin drizzle of chocolate onto your cake or brownies is to put warm melted chocolate into a zip lock bag and cut a tiny hole in one corner. Use it like a pastry/icing bag.

3 ounces of chocolate is ½ cup
4 ounces of chocolate is ¾ cup
6 ounces of chocolate is 1 cup

Most baking chocolate comes in 1–ounce squares.

In a pinch you can use 3 tablespoons cocoa and 1 tablespoon shortening/coconut oil to give you 1 ounce unsweetened chocolate.

If you are adding liquid, at least 1 tablespoon of liquid is needed for every 2 ounces of chocolate (⅓ cup) so seizing doesn't happen. If your chocolate seizes you can either let it dry and wrap it for future use in baking or add more liquid to make a chocolate sauce.

Store your chocolate in airtight containers. Room temperature is ok for most chocolate. Check the recipe if it says differently. 10 days at room temperature is a standard life. Chocolate kept in the fridge will last longer — but you'll want to thaw to room temperature before you eat it.

"What's this weird grey stuff on my chocolate?" Oh dear. You've probably stored your chocolate in damp or warm (over 65° F) conditions. This is the sugar or fat "blooming." It won't ruin your chocolate, but always store in a cool and dry place to avoid it. In these conditions, tightly sealed, your plain solid chocolate will keep about a year.

Chocolate making is a whole science unto itself. I've made these recipes very simple and they don't really delve into that whole world very much. There are plenty of online resources for chocolate making. You can even find hands–on classes put on by chocolate and cake shops.

Chocolate Zucchini Bread

YIELD: ONE LOAF

¼ cup chocolate chips
1½ cups barley flour
2 teaspoons baking powder
1 teaspoon cinnamon
¼ cup cocoa
1 cup sugar
1 cup shredded zucchini
⅓ cup oil
½ cup water
1 teaspoon vanilla
1 tablespoon ground flaxseed mixed with 3 tablespoons water
1 teaspoon vinegar

1. Preheat oven to 350° F. Melt the chocolate chips in a double boiler (or a smaller pot on top of a larger pot of simmering water.)
2. In a large bowl mix the dry ingredients.
3. In a medium bowl mix the wet ingredients including zucchini and melted chocolate.
3. Mix the wet into the dry and pour into greased loaf pan.
4. Bake for about 45 minutes.

Chocolate Coconut Loaf

YIELD: ONE LOAF

1½ cups flour
¾ cup medium-shred coconut
¼ cup cocoa
1 teaspoon baking powder
1 teaspoon baking soda
1 cup soymilk mixed with 1 tablespoon lemon juice
1 cup packed brown sugar
¼ cup oil
¾ cup chocolate chips
3 tablespoons margarine

1. Preheat oven to 350° F. Grease a loaf pan.
2. In a large bowl mix the flour, ½ cup coconut, cocoa, baking powder, and baking soda.
3. In a medium bowl mix the soymilk, sugar and oil. Mix the wet into the dry. Pour into loaf pan.
4. Bake for 40 minutes. Cool.
5. Toast the coconut in a dry pan, mixing constantly until its lightly brown.
6. Melt the chocolate chips in a double boiler with margarine and mix in the coconut. Spread on cake.

Chocolate Orange Millet Cake

YIELD: AN 8–INCH PAN

½ cup millet

1¼ cups water

2 ounces unsweetened chocolate

1 cup wheat–free flour

⅛ cup cocoa

1 teaspoon baking powder

½ cup plus 3 tablespoons maple syrup

⅓ cup orange juice

⅓ cup oil

½ teaspoon orange extract

1 teaspoon vanilla

1. In a medium pot cook the millet in the water for about 30 minutes.
2. Preheat oven to 350° F. Grease an 8–inch pan.
3. Melt the chocolate in a double boiler (or a smaller pot on top of a larger pot of simmering water.)
4. In a large bowl mix the dry ingredients with a whisk. In a small bowl mix the wet ingredients with a whisk until frothy.
5. Mix the wet into the dry and add the cooked millet. Pour into pan and bake for about 30 minutes.

Fabulous Flourless Chocolate Torte

YIELD: 9–INCH PAN

A cross between flourless torte and chocolate potato cake — this is dense, rich, and easy on a digestive system allergic to gluten!

10 ounces unsweetened chocolate
1½ cups ground almonds
1½ cups sugar
1 cup mashed potatoes
½ cup margarine
½ cup tofu
2 tablespoons Dutch cocoa
1 tablespoon vanilla

1. Preheat oven to 350° F. Grease 9–inch springform pan.
2. Melt chocolate in a double boiler (or a smaller pot on top of a larger pot of simmering water)
2. Blend all ingredients together in a processor. Pour into pan and bake for 50 min.

Topping:
3 tablespoons icing sugar
1 tablespoon water
½ cup toasted almond slices

1. Cool cake for 30 minutes. Mix the icing sugar and water.
2. Spread icing sugar mixture on ½ inch around the top rim of the cake and sprinkle nuts, lightly pressing down. You can cover the sides too, just use more icing and almonds.

Peanut Butter Chip Choco Chookies

YIELD: ABOUT 2 DOZEN

There is no doubt that peanut butter and chocolate is the best marriage in the history of cooking. Add a little crunch in the form of a cookie and you'll be saying "just one more."

1⅓ cups chocolate chips
¾ cup brown sugar, packed
¼ cup margarine
¼ cup applesauce
1½ teaspoons vanilla
1½ – 2 cups flour
¼ teaspoon baking powder
¾ cup vegan peanut butter chips
¼ cup natural peanut butter

1. Preheat oven to 300° F. Melt chocolate in double boiler (or smaller pot on top of a larger pot of simmering water) and take off heat.
2. Add the sugar, margarine, applesauce, and vanilla straight to your pot.
3. Mix the flour and baking powder together. Gradually add to the pot, stirring.
4. Make golf ball size dough balls and press flat onto greased baking sheet. Press a little peanut butter into the tops. Bake 16 to 18 minutes, being careful not to burn the bottoms. After removing from oven let cookies sit for a minute and then remove from pan.

Gingerbread Chocolate Cookies

YIELD: 16 LARGE COOKIES

Another inspiration from Columbia, Missouri — this one from Uprise Bakery.
Chocolate and ginger make this a spicy, rich, and soft delight.

1¾ cups flour
¼ cup cocoa
2 teaspoons baking powder
1 teaspoon cinnamon
½ teaspoon nutmeg
½ teaspoon allspice
1½ cups sugar
½ cup plus 2 tablespoons margarine
¼ cup blackstrap molasses
1½ tablespoons fresh ginger
1 cup roughly chopped plain chocolate bar (about 4.5 ounces)
1–3 tablespoons water, if necessary

1. Preheat oven to 325° F.
2. Mix the flour, cocoa, baking powder, and spices in a medium bowl. Cream the margarine and sugar together in a large bowl. Mix in molasses and ginger.
3. Mix the dry into the wet and add the chocolate. Mix into dough ball with your hands. If the dough is much too dry add 1 tablespoon of water at a time. Mix well between each one. The dough is on the dry side, but if it holds together well the consistency is right. Place 16 balls of dough (do not press flat) on an ungreased baking sheet and bake for about 18 minutes.

If you must use cheap, soft margarine you probably won't need any of the additional water.

Flourless Cashew Cookies

YIELD: 15 COOKIES

Both crispy and chewy, you'll love these cookies even if you aren't allergic to peanuts or gluten. Inspired by Sweets From the Earth (www.sweetsfromtheearth.com). They make the best cheezecake ever. I'd swear on my own grave.

1 cup chilled cashew butter
⅓ cup white sugar
⅓ cup brown sugar, packed
2 tablespoons tofu
1 teaspoon vanilla
¼ cup mini semisweet chocolate chips

1. Preheat oven to 350° F.
2. In a processor blend everything well. Incorporate the chocolate chips by processing in a couple short intervals.
3. Spoon heaping tablespoons of the dough onto an ungreased baking sheet. Flatten with a fork in a crisscross pattern.
4. Bake for 16–18 minutes. Let cool for a few minutes on the baking sheet. The cookies are delicate at this point. Carefully transfer onto wire racks to fully cool.

For variation use almond butter and ¼ teaspoon cinnamon.

Auntie Mary's Shortbread

YIELD: AN 8–INCH PAN

Auntie Mary never made the shortbread with chocolate but it was the only way to incorporate this recipe into the book! She also wasn't my aunt, she was my dad's cousin's grandmother. But whoever she was, she made the best shortbread in the world.

½ cup chocolate chips
1¾ cups flour
½ cup rice flour
½ cup cornstarch
½ cup sugar
½ pound good-quality margarine

1. Melt the chocolate over a double boiler (or a small pot on top of a larger pot of simmering water). Cool.
2. Preheat oven to 325° F. Oil an 8–inch pan.
3. Mix all the flours and cornstarch. In a separate bowl cream the sugar and margarine.
4. With your fingers, slowly incorporate the margarine mixture into the flours.
5. As you've added your last piece of margarine, transfer half the mixture to a separate bowl. Pour the chocolate into one.
6. Knead the dough until it forms a ball. Don't over-knead; as soon as it comes together let it be.
7. Carefully press the two dough balls together. Take yourself back to those great days of play dough. You want to have a swirling effect, just a few squeezes and mashes here and there.
8. Press into the pan until it's flat. Take a fork and poke many holes, all the way to the bottom.
9. Bake for about 35 minutes, until the sides/bottom go tan brown in color. Cool for one hour before cutting. Store in tin at room temperature.

Spiced "3 Gram Sugar" Cookies

YIELD: 8 LARGE COOKIES

Since stevia isn't any kind of sugar at all, these dense cookies are very low in sugar content.

⅔ cup kamut flour
⅓ cup barley flour
⅓ cup soy flour
1 teaspoon nutmeg
2 teaspoons vanilla
⅓ cup oil
1 teaspoon liquid stevia
1 tablespoon malt syrup
1 tablespoon agave syrup
2 tablespoons chocolate chips

1. Preheat oven to 300° F.
2. In a medium bowl mix the flours and nutmeg.
3. In a large bowl mix the vanilla, oil, stevia, and syrups.
4. Mix the dry into the wet. Add chocolate chips. Make into dough and split into 8 pieces.
5. On a lightly oiled baking sheet flatten the dough balls and bake for about 30 minutes.
6. Melt chocolate and spread thinly on cookies when they've cooled.

Creem Cheeze Lemon Chocolate Brownie

YIELD: AN 8–INCH PAN

INCREDIBLY *rich. Don't get yourself sick off these.*

Lemon:
2 tablespoons tofu cream cheese
¼ cup fresh lemon juice
3 tablespoons sugar
½ cup firm tofu

Brownie:
5 ounces unsweetened chocolate
1⅔ cups sugar
⅓ cup firm tofu
½ tub tofu cream cheese (4 ounces)
¾ cup flour less 2 tablespoons
½ teaspoon baking powder
pinch of salt
½ cup semisweet chocolate chips, melted

1. Blend all the lemon ingredients and set aside.
2. Melt brownie chocolate in double boiler (or a small pot on top of a larger pot of simmering water.)
3. Preheat oven to 350° F. Blend the sugar, tofu and tofu cream cheese. Add the melted brownie chocolate and blend again. Pour into a large bowl.
4. Mix the flour, baking powder, and salt in a medium bowl. Mix the dry into the wet.
5. Pour into 8–inch pan and pour the lemon concoction on top. Bake for about 50 minutes.
6. Zig-zag your melted chocolate on top of the cooling brownies.

Pinwheel Cookies

YIELD: 2 DOZEN SMALL COOKIES

These fun-looking cookies seem to come out only during holidays. Don't let the steps involved scare you — it's actually very easy — keep a picture of the final product in your mind.

Wax paper

¾ cup sugar
½ cup margarine
4 tablespoons water
2 teaspoons vanilla
1½ cup flour
dash of salt
2 tablespoons cocoa
2 tablespoons oil

1. Cream the sugar with margarine and water until fluffy. Mix in vanilla.
2. Add flour and salt and mix. Before dough begins to take shape divide mixture in half. Take one half and add the cocoa and oil. Knead each dough ball separately.
3. Wrap the dough in plastic and refrigerate 30 minutes.
4. On two pieces of wax paper roll out the two pieces of dough to approximately 16 x 16–inch. If you have problems with the dough crumbling keep patting flat with your hand. Invert the white dough onto the chocolate dough and peel off the top wax paper.
5. Begin rolling the dough lengthwise like a jellyroll, removing the wax paper on the bottom of the chocolate as you go. Beware of crumbling dough. Wrap in plastic and refrigerate 30 minutes.
6. Preheat oven to 400° F. With a sharp knife slice the roll into ¼–inch pieces. If the dough becomes too soft when you are slicing put it back into the fridge for a few minutes. If the cookies are falling apart gently squeeze them together.
7. Bake the cookies on an ungreased sheet for 6–8 minutes or until lightly browned on bottom.

Creem Topping

YIELD: 2½ CUPS

A mousse–like concoction that can be scooped on top of cake or hot chocolate.

Food processor or Vitamix

2 cups soymilk
⅓ teaspoon agar powder
¼ cup plus 2 tablespoons sugar
2 teaspoons vanilla
½ cup tofu
2 tablespoons oil

1. Mix the soymilk, agar, and sugar in a small pot and simmer a couple minutes, whisking quickly and constantly. It's all about the foam!
2. In a food processor blend the tofu. Blend in the soymilk mixture and vanilla at high speed — leave any stoppers off the lid so air can get in. Add the oil in a thin stream while blending.
3. Blend this mixture a bit longer to incorporate air. Cover and chill.
4. When ready to use you will find your creem topping to be a solid chunk. Mix it up a bit with a whisk if using on a cake or blend well with other ingredients if incorporating in some other dessert.

A Vitamix works well for this recipe due to the large opening at the top. To get a light foam topping, remelt the chilled creem topping (with a little extra liquid to help it along). Whisk quickly and continually. Chill again. The foam rises to the top and a pudding–like mix sits on the bottom. You'll get maybe a ½ cup of foam from this recipe.

German Chocolate Cake

YIELD: 8–9-INCH CAKE

According to a German, this cake is not really German. But the Black Forest one is — so if you want to impress German friends you can make that one or call this cake by another name!

Parchment paper

¾ cup semisweet chocolate chips
½ cup boiling water
½ cup chilled oil
½ cup margarine
2 cups sugar
4 tablespoons ground flaxseed mixed with ½ cup + 2 tablespoons water
1 teaspoon vanilla
2½ cups flour
1 teaspoon baking soda
1 teaspoon baking powder
pinch of salt
1 cup soymilk mixed with 1 tablespoon lemon juice

Topping:
3 tablespoons ground flaxseed mixed with 6 tablespoons soymilk
¼ cup margarine
⅓ cup sugar
⅓ cup soy yogurt
1 teaspoon vanilla
1⅓ cups medium shredded coconut
1 cup chopped pecans

Frosting:
3 tablespoons margarine
3 ounces unsweetened chocolate, melted
1 teaspoon vanilla
2 cups icing sugar, sifted
4 tablespoons soymilk

1. In a small pot melt chocolate by mixing with the 1/2 cup boiling water and heating on low; let cool.
2. Line the bottom of three 8 or 9–inch pans with parchment paper. In a very large bowl cream the oil, margarine and sugar until fluffy.
3. Preheat oven to 350° F. Add the ground flax mixture and vanilla to the sugar. Mix in the chocolate.
4. Sift the flour, baking soda, baking powder, and salt into a large bowl. Alternately add this and the soymilk to the chocolate/sugar mixture, beating smooth after each addition.
5. Pour into pans and bake 30 to 40 minutes. Arrange the pans the best you can in the oven: not touching each other or the sides of the oven. Cool, turn out onto wire racks to cool further.
6. Prepare the topping: In a medium pot stir everything but coconut and pecans over medium heat until thickened. Remove from heat. Stir in coconut and pecans and cool, beating occasionally. Spread on top of each cake layer, reserving a little more for the top.
7. Prepare the frosting: Mix the margarine, chocolate, and vanilla into the icing sugar. Add enough soymilk to make the frosting spreadable.

Black Forest Cake

YIELD: 8–9–INCH CAKE

Electric mixer
Pastry/icing bag
Parchment paper

1½ cups soymilk
1 tablespoon vinegar
1⅔ cups flour
⅔ cup cocoa
1½ teaspoons baking soda
dash of salt
1½ cups sugar
½ cup oil
1 teaspoon vanilla
2 15 or 16 ounce cans black cherries in syrup
¼ cup icing sugar
2 tablespoons arrowroot
3 cups Creem Topping (page 91), or soy whipped cream
1 ounce square semisweet chocolate

1. Mix the soymilk with the vinegar and let sit.
2. Grease 3 8-inch cake pans. Put parchment paper at the bottom. Preheat oven to 350° F.
3. In a large bowl sift the flour, cocoa, baking soda, and salt. Add sugar and mix with a whisk.
4. In a separate bowl mix the soymilk, oil, and vanilla and whisk until foamy. Pour the liquid into the flour mixture and quickly mix until smooth. Pour evenly into the 3 pans. Smooth with spoon to make flat. Arrange the pans the best you can in the oven: not touching each other or the sides of the oven.
5. Bake for about 20 minutes or until a toothpick comes out cleanly. Cool, turn out onto wire racks to cool for a further 10 minutes. Wrap in plastic and refrigerate.
6. Sift together icing sugar and arrowroot. In a large bowl with electric mixers beat sugar/arrowroot into creem topping.
7. Drain canned cherries, keeping ¾ cup of juice. Place a cake layer on a plate and poke it with a fork in about 15 places. Carefully spoon on ⅓ of the juice. Put about ¾ cup creem topping on the layer. Fork holes in the second layer and place on top of the first layer. BE CAREFUL — the cake is delicate. Spoon another ⅓ of juice on this layer and top with creem topping. Fork holes and place the final layer, spooning on the remainder of the juice. Top with most of the cherries, leaving ½-inch ring around edges. Frost the sides of the cake and use a pastry bag to pipe around the last ½-inch ring on the top. Chill.
8. Grate the chocolate and press into sides of cake.

Cinnamon Chocolate Sour Creem Cake

YIELD: 10–12–INCH BUNDT PAN

*This cake is really nice. The cinnamon adds a little surprise
to people just expecting regular chocolate cake.*

Sour Creem:
1 cup firm silken tofu
¼ cup lemon juice
¼ cup oil
dash of salt

Cake:
½ cup margarine
½ cup oil
2 cups sugar
¼ cup + 2 tablespoons ground flaxseed mixed with 1 cup water
1 teaspoon vanilla
1 teaspoon baking powder
1 teaspoon baking soda
2¾ cups flour
½ cup cocoa
3 teaspoons cinnamon

1. Preheat oven to 325° F. Grease a 10 or 12–inch tube (bundt) pan.
2. In a large bowl cream the margarine, oil, and sugar until fluffy. Add the flax/water mixture and vanilla,
   mixing well.
3. In another large bowl sift and mix the dry ingredients.
4. Add the dry mix to the wet bowl, alternately with the sour creem and beating after each addition.
5. Pour into pan and bake approximately 1 hour and 5 minutes. Cool for about 15 minutes in the pan,
   then turn out onto a rack to cool completely.

For variety frost with Banana Cinnamon Buttercreem (page 121).

Ginger Cake

YIELD: AN 8–9–INCH PAN

Inspired by an incredible and memorable piece of chocolate-covered ginger at a New Years party in 2000.

Parchment Paper

3 cups flour
3½ teaspoons ginger
1½ teaspoons baking powder
1½ cups brown sugar, packed
1 cup water
⅔ cup oil
½ cup applesauce
⅓ cup rice syrup
1–inch fresh ginger (about 2 tablespoons)
2 ounces unsweetened chocolate
4 tablespoons boiling water
3 tablespoons margarine
1 cup icing sugar

1. Preheat oven to 350° F. Lay parchment paper on the bottom of two 8– or 9–inch pans. Oil the sides.
2. Sift and mix the flour, ginger, and baking powder in a large bowl. In a medium bowl mix the sugar, water, oil, and applesauce with a whisk until foamy.
3. Pour wet into dry, stirring quickly until smooth. Bake for about 25 minutes until toothpick comes out clean. Cool on wire racks.
4. Boil the rice syrup and fresh ginger in a pot for 3 minutes. Cool until warm. Turn out cooled cakes and poke each with fork about 30 times. Discard the ginger. Pour the syrup over the top and let sink in.
5. Melt the chocolate in a double boiler (or medium pot on top of larger pot of simmering water.) Add the boiling water and margarine. Stir in icing sugar until smooth. Pour ⅓ on the bottom layer cake. Place the second layer and add the rest of the chocolate glaze. Let drip over the side.

If you are a strong person or want this cake to kick your butt, try another couple teaspoons of ground ginger in the cake mixture.

Maple Pecan Fudge Cake

YIELD: AN 9–INCH CAKE

Cake:
2 cups mixed wheat-free flour (I used 1 cup oat and 1 cup barley)
½ cup cocoa
½ cup ground pecans
2 teaspoons baking powder
1⅓ cups maple syrup
½ cup oil
½ cup soymilk
2 teaspoons vanilla

Ganache middle:
1 cup chocolate chips
¼ cup margarine
3 tablespoons soymilk
¼ cup chopped pecans

Maple Buttercream Frosting (page 121):
10 whole pecan halves to garnish

1. Preheat oven to 350° F. Grease two 8– or 9–inch cake pans.
2. In a large bowl mix the dry ingredients together. In a medium bowl whisk the wet together.
3. Mix the wet into the dry and pour into pans. Bake about 30 minutes.
4. When cake is cooled melt the chocolate chips in a double boiler and add the margarine and soymilk. Mix well, then add the chopped pecans. Put this chocolate filling on the top of one cake and gently place the second layer on top.
5. Frost the cake and arrange whole pecan halves in whatever design you wish.

If you eliminate the ganache middle and frosting, you have a cake that's not so bad for you.

The Stupid Canuck 2–Sided Cake

YIELD: AN 8–INCH PAN

Chocolate, vanilla, strawberries, and coconut.
Concocted on a Canada Day while in a very mixed-up state.

2 cups sliced strawberries
1½ cups flour
½ cup cocoa
½ cup white sugar
½ cup brown sugar, packed
2 teaspoons baking powder
1 cup soymilk
½ cup oil
¼ cup water
1½ teaspoon vanilla

Topping:
1 cup coconut
½ cup icing sugar
3 tablespoons margarine
2 tablespoons soymilk
1 teaspoon vanilla

1. Place sliced strawberries at bottom of greased 8–inch cake pan. Preheat oven to 350° F.
2. In a large bowl mix the dry ingredients.
3. In a medium bowl mix the wet ingredients.
4. Mix the wet into the dry and pour into pan. Bake for 30 minutes.
5. For the topping mix all of the ingredients together in a small bowl. When cake is done, spread topping thinly on top. Broil for about 1½ minutes or until lightly browned.

Free Free Chocolate Loaf

YIELD: ONE LOAF PAN

Free of sugar and free of wheat, low in fat, and low in gluten.
This is one of the few healthy recipes in the bunch.

1¾ cups barley flour
4 tablespoons Dutch cocoa
2 teaspoons baking powder
1 teaspoon cinnamon
¼ teaspoon cardamom
dash of salt
⅓ cup rice syrup
¼ cup applesauce
1 cup soymilk
1¾ teaspoons liquid stevia
¼ cup oil

1. Preheat oven to 350° F. Grease a loaf pan.
2. In a large bowl mix the dry ingredients.
3. In a small bowl mix the wet ingredients.
4. Mix wet into dry and pour into pan.
5. Bake 40 minutes.

Chocolate Bourbon Pecan Pie

YIELD: 9–INCH PIE

This recipe, also known as "Better Than Sex Pie" in some circles, comes from the lovely ladies of How It All Vegan *and* Garden of Vegan. *govegan.net*

egg replacer equal to 2 eggs
2 tablespoons blackstrap molasses
½ cup corn syrup
2 tablespoons bourbon (or ½ teaspoon rum extract)
1 teaspoon vanilla extract
½ teaspoon salt
1 ½ cups pecans, chopped
1 cup chocolate chips
4 whole pecan halves
1 pie crust

1. Preheat oven to 350° F.
2. In a bowl combine egg replacer, molasses, corn syrup, bourbon or extract, vanilla, and salt. Add chopped pecans and chocolate chips and mix well.
3. Pour into pie crust and arrange pecan halves on top in the center. Bake for 40–45 minutes.

Cows of Guelph Cake

YIELD: AN 8-INCH PAN

Guelph, Ontario, is a cute little college town surrounded by fields.
This is another funny recipe made at Michele and Sarah's.

1½ cups flour
1 cup sugar
1½ teaspoons baking powder
1 cup water
⅓ cup oil
1 teaspoon vanilla
½ cup cocoa, sifted
3 tablespoons soymilk

1. Preheat oven to 350° F. Grease an 8-inch pan.
2. In a large bowl mix the flour, ¾ cup sugar, and 1¼ teaspoons baking powder. Mix the water, oil, and vanilla in a separate bowl.
3. In another bowl mix cocoa, ½ teaspoon baking powder, ¼ cup of sugar, and soymilk. You'll have to work quickly from this point.
4. Mix the wet into the dry from instruction #2. Save ½ cup batter.
5. Pour the vanilla batter into a pan and tilt to even out. Beat the cocoa mixture into the ½ cup batter.
6. Dollop cocoa mixture onto the surface of the vanilla batter in cow patterned blobs — about 2 tablespoons of cocoa dolloped into 4 blobs.
7. Bake for approximately 35 minutes. Toothpick should come out dry in the vanilla cake.

For a Big Cow Cake, double the recipe and bake in a 9 x 13-inch pan. Eat with chocolate chip ice creem (page 144)

Autumn Drop Cake

YIELD: AN 8–INCH CAKE

A Halloween cake for the Ranch in Columbia, Missouri.

Thermometer

3 cups flour
2 teaspoons baking powder
1 teaspoon baking soda
2 teaspoons pumpkin pie spice
pinch of salt
1½ cups sugar
⅓ cup brown sugar, packed
⅓ cup oil
⅓ cup margarine
½ teaspoon vanilla
1 cup canned pumpkin
1⅓ cups soymilk mixed with 1 tablespoon vinegar
½ cup mini semisweet chocolate chips

Frosting:
3 cups sugar
2 cups soymilk
¼ cup margarine
¼ cup canned pumpkin
1 teaspoon pumpkin pie spice

1. Preheat oven to 350° F. Grease two 8–inch pans.
2. In a large bowl sift flour, baking powder, baking soda, spice, and salt. Stir with whisk.
3. In a small bowl, cream the sugars, oil, and margarine together. Add vanilla, pumpkin, and soymilk.
4. Mix the wet into the dry, add chocolate chips, and pour into pans. Smooth top. Bake for approximately 40 minutes until toothpick comes out clean.
5. Cool cakes on racks for 10 minutes. Remove cakes from pans and cool for another 10 minutes.
6. Prepare frosting. Boil the soymilk and sugar until it reaches 230° F. Take off heat and add spice, margarine and pumpkin. Let cool to about 110° F (warm to touch) and beat with wooden spoon.

Chocolate Malt Cake

YIELD: 8–9–INCH PAN

Jonathan is crazy about chocolate malt shakes
and it gave me idea to turn this combo into a cake.

1¾ cups sugar
½ cup margarine
½ cup oil
1 cup soymilk mixed with 1 tablespoon lemon juice
¼ cup + 2 tablespoons ground flaxseed mixed with 1 cup water
2 teaspoons vanilla
2¾ cups flour
½ cup cocoa
½ cup malt powder
1 teaspoon baking powder
1 teaspoon baking soda

Frosting:
3 cups icing sugar
⅔ cup cocoa
½ cup malt powder
½ cup + 2 tablespoons margarine
2 tablespoons + 4 teaspoons soymilk

1. Preheat oven to 350° F. Grease two or three 8 or 9–inch pans.
2. In a large bowl, cream the sugar, margarine, and oil. Mix in the soymilk, flax/water, and vanilla.
3. In a separate bowl sift the flour, cocoa, malt powder, baking powder, and baking soda. Stir with whisk.
4. Mix the wet into the dry to make a smooth batter. Pour into pans and bake 35 minutes if 3 pans and about 1 hour with two.
5. To make frosting, first mix the dry ingredients together in a large bowl. Add the margarine (mixture will still be dry) and enough soymilk to make a smooth spreading frosting. Frost the top, middle, and sides of the cooled cake.

Toll–Free Chocolate Chip Cookies

YIELD: 24–28 COOKIES

Your traditional rich and yummy chocolate chip cookie without the animal products.

1 cup margarine
¾ cup white sugar
¾ cup brown sugar
2 tablespoons ground flaxseed mixed with 4 tablespoons water
½ teaspoon vanilla
2 cups flour
2 cups semisweet chocolate chips
1 teaspoon baking soda
dash of salt

1. Preheat oven to 350° F.
2. In a large bowl cream the margarine and sugars. Add the flax mixture and vanilla and cream until fluffy.
3. In a medium bowl mix the flour, chocolate chips, baking soda, and salt.
4. Mix the dry into the wet. Form dough into walnut-sized pieces and place on ungreased baking sheets. Leave at least 2 inches of space in between. Bake for about 13 minutes. Loosen cookies on sheet after a few minutes so they don't stick.

Chocolate Chip Tofu Cheezecake

YIELD: A 9–INCH PAN

Unlike the cheezecake in my previous book,
this one is very cheap to make yet still tastes delish.

Chocolate Cookie Crust:
1¼ cups chocolate cookie crumbs
3 tablespoons oil

Filling:
2 12.3-ounce packages firm silken tofu
1 cup sugar
½ cup oil
¼ cup arrowroot starch mixed with ¼ cup soymilk
¼ cup lemon juice
1 teaspoon almond extract
1 tablespoon vanilla extract
⅓ cup chopped chocolate chips

1. Mix the ground cookies with oil and press into bottom of a 9–inch springform pan. Bake at 375° F for 8 minutes. Reduce heat to 350° F.
2. Blend all the cheesecake ingredients except the chocolate chips. Mix in the chips and pour into baked crust.
3. Bake about 55 minutes until the middle is very nearly set.
4. Cool and remove the springform pan.

Double-Decker Chocolate Mint Cheezecake

YIELD: 8 OR 9–INCH PIE

½ cup chocolate chips
1 tub vegan cream cheese (8 ounces)
1 cup firm tofu
¾ cup soy yogurt
¾ cup sugar
¼ cup flour
egg replacer equivalent to 2 eggs
1 teaspoon vanilla
pinch of salt
2 tablespoons crushed candy cane
¼ teaspoon mint extract
chocolate cookie crust (page 105)

1. Preheat oven to 325° F. Melt chocolate in a double boiler (or a smaller pot on top of a larger pot of simmering water.)
2. Blend all ingredients except candy cane, mint extract and chocolate.
3. Take out ⅓ of this mix. Add the melted chocolate to the ⅔ still in the blender and blend well.
4. Pour the chocolate into the pie crust. Mix the candy cane and mint extract into the remaining ⅓ mixture and pour this on top of the chocolate. Bake for 50 minutes.

Oatmeal Pie Crust

YIELD: ONE 8–9–INCH PIE

2 cups quick-cooking oats
⅓ cup melted margarine
3 tablespoons agave syrup
dash of salt

1. Preheat oven to 375° F.
2. Combine oats with margarine and add the rest. Press into a greased pie plate and bake for 15 to 20 minutes.

Coconut Chocolate Pie Crust

YIELD: 8–9-INCH PIE

2 ounces unsweetened chocolate
2 tablespoons margarine
⅔ cup icing sugar
2 tablespoons hot water
1½ cups large shred coconut

1. Grease a pie plate. In a medium pot melt the chocolate and margarine together on low.
2. Mix the icing sugar and water together. Add to chocolate mix. Add coconut and stir well.
3. Press into the pie plate and chill until set.

Nut Pie Crust

YIELD: A 9–INCH PIE

1 cup almonds, pecans, walnuts or combination
⅓ cup chocolate chips
2 tablespoons margarine
2 tablespoons soymilk
¾ cup sifted icing sugar

1. Blend the nuts until finely chopped. Grease a 9-inch pie pan.
2. In a medium pot melt the chocolate with margarine and soymilk. Stir in icing sugar.
   Press into pan and chill.

Chocolate Caramel Pecan Rolls

YIELD: 24 ROLLS

Electric mixer

Rolls:
1¾ cups soymilk
½ cup water
5 tablespoons margarine
4 tablespoons brown sugar
¼ cup white sugar
1½ teaspoons salt
2 packages of yeast
2 squares unsweetened chocolate, melted
5 cups flour
½ cup cocoa

Caramel:
1½ cup brown sugar, packed
½ cup margarine
1 cup roughly chopped pecans

Filling:
2 tablespoons margarine
½ cup chopped pecans
¼ cup brown sugar

1. Combine soymilk, water, margarine, brown sugar, white sugar, and salt in a pot on medium heat and dissolve. Pour into a bowl and cool until temperature is warm. Sprinkle the yeast on top, mix a bit, and then let sit in warm place for about 10 minutes.
2. Add melted chocolate, 2 cups of flour, and cocoa. With an electric mixer beat on low for 30 seconds then beat on high speed for 3 more minutes.
3. Stir in enough flour to make a soft dough. Knead for 5 minutes. Turn into a greased bowl, cover, and let rise in a warm place for about 30 minutes.
4. Melt the margarine and brown sugar in a pot on medium to make the caramel. Simmer for a few minutes. Pour into the bottom of three 8 or 9–inch round pans. Sprinkle 1 cup chopped pecans evenly between the pans.

5. Divide dough into two portions. Roll them to 10 x 12–inch rectangles. Dot margarine, sprinkle brown sugar and chopped pecans. Roll into jellyrolls. With a very sharp knife cut into 24 pieces and put 8 pieces in each cake pan.

6. Chill for 2 to 24 hours. Thaw 30 minutes before baking. Bake at 350° F for 30 minutes. Overturn onto plate. Let caramel drip on top…

Frozen Chocolate Bananas

YIELD: 6 PIECES

Wax or parchment paper
6 skewers

6 peeled bananas
1 cup chocolate chips
¼ cup margarine
3 tablespoons soymilk
⅓ cup finely chopped nuts or coconut

1. Line a baking sheet with wax or parchment paper. In a large pot melt the chocolate, margarine, and soymilk.

2. Skewer the bananas and dip in chocolate. Cover completely. Dip into nuts or coconut.

3. Freeze. Eat or wrap in foil and keep in freezer. Let sit room temperature a few minutes before eating.

You can liven up these old-fashioned concoctions by rolling in cookie or brownie crumbs, toasted coconut, sprinkles, or candy pieces.

Tundra Bars

YIELD: A 9X12–INCH PAN

People like to talk about the tundra in northern Canada.
These bars are named after that snow-covered, treeless, moss-sprouting land.

Bottom:
½ cup natural peanut butter
⅓ cup packed brown sugar
¼ cup margarine
1 cup spelt flour

Top:
2 tablespoons ground flaxseed mixed with 6 tablespoons water
1 teaspoon vanilla
1 cup chocolate chips
¾ cup shredded coconut
½ cup packed brown sugar
2 tablespoons spelt flour
1 teaspoon baking powder
pinch of salt

1. Preheat oven to 350° F. In a medium bowl mix the peanut butter, sugar, and margarine.
   Add the flour. Spread into an ungreased 9 x 12–inch pan — it will be thin. Bake 10 minutes.
2. In a medium bowl mix the flax, vanilla, and sugar. Add the chocolate chips, coconut, brown sugar,
   flour, baking powder and salt. Mix well and spread on top of crust. Bake 15 minutes.
   Cool and cut into bars.

Chocolate-Covered Gingerbread Cookies

3 cups flour
1 tablespoon ginger
1 teaspoon cinnamon
½ teaspoon cloves
½ teaspoon baking soda
2 cups sugar
⅔ cup oil
½ cup blackstrap molasses
⅓ cup + 1 tablespoon water
½ teaspoon vinegar
2 cups chocolate chips
1–2 teaspoons ginger (optional)

1. Mix the flour with spices and baking soda in a medium bowl.
2. Preheat the oven to 300° F. In a large bowl cream the sugar, oil, molasses, water, and vinegar.
3. Mix the dry into the wet and form a dough. Roll out to about ¼–inch thick. Cut out with cookie cutters. Feet, airplanes, stars — something fun.
4. Bake for 7–15 minutes depending on the size of the cutter. Remember that cookies continue to cook on the pan after you take them out.
5. Melt chocolate with optional ginger in a double boiler (or small pot on top of larger pot of simmering water.) Cover tops of cooled cookie with melted chocolate by dipping in pot and swirling around. Chill.

Chocolate-Topped Shortbread Cookies

YIELD: ABOUT 25 1½-INCH COOKIES

There was a place in Kensington Market (in Toronto) that sold these weird and yummy-flavored shortbread cookies. They were the inspiration behind these recipes. Flavor increases with time.

Orange Cardamom:
2 cups flour
1 teaspoon cardamom
1 cup margarine (good quality)
⅔ cup sugar
¾ teaspoons orange extract

1. Mix the flour and cardamom in a large bowl.
2. Mix the sugar and margarine in a small bowl. Add the orange extract.
3. Mix the wet into the dry until you get a dough. Chill for 30 minutes.
4. Preheat oven to 350° F and roll the dough to ½ inch thick between two pieces of wax paper. Use a small size cookie cutter and place on ungreased baking sheet. Bake 20–25 minutes until bottoms lightly brown.
5. Top with melted chocolate.

Lemon Anise:
Omit the cardamom and replace the orange extract with
½ teaspoon lemon extract and ¼ teaspoon anise extract

Ginger Coriander:
Omit the orange extract and replace the cardamom with
½ teaspoon ginger and ½ teaspoon ground coriander

Nutmeg Hazelnut:
1⅓ cups flour
¾ cup ground hazelnuts
½ teaspoon nutmeg
½ teaspoon vanilla
Note: Cut out ⅔ cup of flour and add the ground hazelnuts instead.
Replace cardamom with nutmeg and orange extract with vanilla.

Maggot Bars

YIELD: AN 8-INCH PAN

*Maybe you'd prefer to call them Puffed Rice Bars or something of the sort,
but they're a healthy treat for kids who'd have fun eating them called by the right name.*

½ cup natural peanut butter
½ cup maple syrup
2 tablespoons cocoa
dash of salt
3 cups puffed (not crisped) rice

1. In a large pot melt the peanut butter with the maple syrup on low heat. Add the cocoa and salt. Mix well.
2. Mix in the puffed rice. Pat into a greased 8-inch pan and chill.

Ci Ci C Bars

YIELD: AN 8-INCH PAN

¾ cup brown sugar, packed
¼ cup oil
1 tablespoon ground flaxseed mixed with 3 tablespoons water
1 cup medium shred coconut
¾ cup barley flour
½ cup chopped walnuts
1 teaspoon baking powder
⅔ cup chocolate chips

1. Preheat oven to 350° F.
2. Mix the sugar, oil, and flax/water. Add the coconut, flour, nuts, and baking powder.
3. Pat into a greased 8-inch pan and bake for 25–30 minutes.
4. Cool bars and melt chocolate in a double boiler. Spread on top of bars. Chill.

Turtle Torte

YIELD: A 9–INCH CAKE

You don't need much of this to be satisfied.

Pasty Brush
Wax paper

Crust:
1 cup plus 2 tablespoons flour
3 tablespoons cocoa
pinch of salt
¼ cup sugar
½ teaspoon vanilla
4 tablespoons ground flaxseed mixed with 6 tablespoons water
4 tablespoons oil

Topping:
1¼ cups chopped pecans
1 cup chocolate chips
¾ cup plus 1 tablespoon soymilk
3 tablespoons oil

Caramel:
1 cup + 3 tablespoons sugar
¼ cup water
⅛ teaspoon salt
2 tablespoons margarine
1 teaspoon vanilla

1. In a large bowl sift the flour, cocoa, and salt. Mix in sugar.
2. Mix the vanilla with the flax mixture. Add this and 4 tablespoons oil to flour. Stir into dough, cover with plastic wrap and chill 30 minutes.
2. Preheat oven to 350° F. Toast the pecans for about 10 minutes. Chop the chocolate chips. Set these aside.
3. Blend the soymilk and oil.

3. Roll out the dough to fit a greased 9–inch springform pan. Place in pan and make sure there is an even lip around the whole thing. With a fork poke the dough. Cut out a piece of wax paper to place on the bottom and put dry beans or rice to weigh and flatten dough. Bake for 20 minutes.

4. Remove the wax paper and the beans/rice. Bake for 10 minutes more. Cool on rack.

5. To make caramel: place sugar, water, and salt in a pot and boil on medium heat until dark amber color. Do not stir, instead swirl around. Use a wet brush to wash down the sugar crystals.

6. Remove from heat and add ½ cup soymilk/oil mixture from the topping ingredients, margarine, and vanilla. Stir until smooth. Pour into pie shell and sprinkle pecans. Chill.

7. In a medium pot boil the rest of the soymilk/oil mixture, turn off heat, and add chocolate. Let sit a few minutes. Stir until smooth and pour over pecans. Chill at least an hour.

Chocolate Sandwiches

YIELD: ABOUT 14 COOKIES

2 cups flour
1 cup sugar
1 teaspoon baking soda
pinch of salt
¼ cup cocoa
1 cup chocolate soymilk
⅓ cup oil
1½ teaspoons vanilla
⅓ cup margarine
1 cup icing sugar
½ cup Ricemellow Creme

1. Preheat oven to 325° F and grease 2–4 baking sheets.
2. In a large bowl mix the flour, sugar, baking soda, salt, and sift in cocoa.
3. Make a well in the above and add the soymilk, oil, and 1 teaspoon vanilla. Mix until smooth.
4. In heaping tablespoonfuls put dough onto baking sheets, leaving 2 inches in between. Bake 10 to 12 minutes.
5. Make filling with an electric mixer if you have one, or just beat with fork: ½ teaspoon vanilla, margarine, icing sugar, and Ricemellow Creme.
6. Spread filling on one cookie, top with a second.

To make strawberry filling use Strawberry Ricemellow Creme, minus vanilla. To make peanut butter filling add ¼ cup natural peanut butter and a dash of salt.

Chocolate Marshmallow Almond Pie

YIELD: A 9–INCH PIE

9–inch pie shell, prebaked
¾ cup sliced almonds
2 teaspoons sugar
1 teaspoon cinnamon
1 cup soymilk
3 tablespoons firm tofu
2 tablespoons oil
½ teaspoon agar powder
1¼ cups Ricemellow Creme
1¼ cups chocolate chips

1. Preheat oven to 300° F. Mix ½ cup almonds with sugar and cinnamon. Toast for about 15 minutes, stirring every once in a while.
2. Blend the soymilk, tofu, oil, and agar until smooth and frothy.
3. Melt the Ricemellow and chocolate chips over a double boiler (or medium pot on top of a larger simmer pot of water.) Set aside.
4. Place the toasted almonds at the bottom of your prebaked pie crust.
5. In a small pot heat the soymilk/agar mixture on low until boiling and thick. Add to chocolate mixture, mixing very well. Pour into pie crust.
6. Sprinkle the remaining ¼ cup almonds on top of pie and chill. Finish by dolloping a few tablespoons of Ricemellow on top of pie.

Chocolate Dulce de Batata Puffs

YIELD: 15 PASTRIES

White folks might be a little confused about this, but I assure you — sweet potato jam is delish! It can be found in Mexican, South American, and Middle Eastern food stores.

Muffin tins

1 box vegan puff pastry (blocks rather than sheets)
1 one–pound tin dulce de batata (sweet potato jam)
2 tablespoons soymilk
6 ounces chocolate chips (1 cup)

1. Thaw the puff pastry for 40 minutes.
2. Blend 1 cup dulce de batata with soymilk until smooth.
3. Preheat oven to 400° F. Roll out one piece of puff pastry so it's 9 x 18–inch. Cut into 15 squares. Place into muffin tins.
4. Put 2 teaspoons dulce de batata mixture and 1 teaspoon chocolate chips in each cups.
5. Bake for 12 minutes. Remove from oven, swirl the chocolate into the sweet potato, and let cool 10 minutes in tin.
6. Remove from tin and cool further on wire racks.

S'more Bars

YIELD: AN 8–INCH PAN

*Franco is really picky about his food and isn't so adventurous in
the nosh department, but he likes these quite a lot!*

⅓ cup margarine
¾ cup sugar
1 tablespoon ground flaxseed with 6 tablespoons water
1 tablespoon blackstrap molasses
1 teaspoon vanilla
1½ cups flour
1 teaspoon baking soda
pinch of salt
¾ cup chocolate chips
1½ cups Ricemellow Creme

1. Grease 8–inch pan and preheat oven to 350° F.
2. In a large bowl cream the margarine and sugar. Add the flax/water mixture, molasses, and vanilla.
3. In a separate bowl mix the flour, baking soda, and salt and add to margarine bowl.
   Mix well into a dough.
4. Pat half of the dough into the pan, pat the chocolate chips onto the dough. Spread the Ricemellow
   Creme on top of the chocolate.
5. Take the rest of the dough by the palm full. Pat in your hand and place on top of the marshmallow in
   sections — they will magically join together in the oven. Bake for 25 minutes.

Turtle Bars

YIELD: A 9–INCH PAN

Bottom:
1½ cups flour
¾ cup brown sugar, lightly packed
½ cup margarine
⅔ cup chopped pecans

Top:
½ cup margarine
⅓ cup brown sugar, packed
¾ cup chocolate chips

1. Preheat oven to 350° F.
2. Make the bottom crust: in a medium bowl mix the flour and brown sugar. Blend in margarine.
   A pastry blender is good for this. Mix until crumbly and even. Pat into an ungreased 9–inch pan.
   Sprinkle the pecans on top.
3. For the topping: in a medium pot, melt margarine and brown sugar until bubbly and simmer
   1 minute, stirring constantly. Remove from heat and pour gently onto pecans.
4. Bake for about 30 minutes. Sprinkle with chocolate chips immediately out of the oven.
   Let stand so they melt a bit and then swirl with a knife.

Chocolate Napoleons

YIELD: 18 SMALL PASTRIES

With the help of custard powder, you can now enjoy these creamy delicacies without milk or eggs. In the U.S. custard powder can be found in specialty shops including British and East Indian.

1 package of vegan puff pastry sheets
1½ cups soymilk
¼ cup sugar
1½ tablespoons margarine
1 ounce square unsweetened chocolate, chopped
3 tablespoons custard powder
½ cup sifted icing sugar
1 tablespoon water
1 ounce semisweet chocolate (3 tablespoon chocolate chips)

1. Thaw one sheet — half a package — of puff pastry for 40 minutes.
2. In a small pot on low heat boil 1 cup soymilk with sugar, margarine, and unsweetened chocolate. Stir to prevent burning.
3. In a separate bowl mix the custard powder into the remaining ½ cup soymilk.
4. When the chocolate has totally melted and incorporated into the soymilk, whisk in the custard powder. Simmer a few minutes, stirring constantly, then pour into a bowl and chill.
5. Preheat oven to 400° F. Cut the pastry down the three fold lines. Then cut each piece into six pieces. You will have a total of 18. Bake for 15 minutes or until golden brown.
6. Cool pastry on racks. Mix the icing sugar with the water. When the custard is chilled and firm cut the pastries in half. Place custard on one side and glaze the tops with icing. Place tops onto custard.
7. Melt the chocolate and spoon into ziplock bag. Cut a very small tip from the bag and drizzle this chocolate onto the iced tops.

Napoleons are one of my favorite pastries, so I went all the way with the icing and the drizzled chocolate. If you can't be bothered, just sift icing sugar on top.

Maple Buttercreem Frosting

YIELD: ABOUT 2½ CUPS

Electric mixer

8 teaspoons flour
¾ cup plus 8 teaspoons soymilk
¼ cup plus 1 tablespoon maple syrup
½ cup sugar
dash of salt
1 teaspoon vanilla
½ cup margarine

1. In a small bowl mix flour gradually with 8 teaspoons soymilk. Make sure there are no lumps and make a smooth paste. Mix in 1 tablespoon maple syrup and the rest of the soymilk.
2. In a small pot cook over medium heat until it becomes a thick paste. Cool.
3. Beat the rest of the syrup, sugar, salt, vanilla, and margarine with an electric mixer until creamy.
4. Gradually add the cooled flour mixture and beat until fluffy and well combined. It might take a while as the fat likes to separate.

Banana Cinnamon Buttercreem Frosting

YIELD: ABOUT 2½ CUPS

Electric mixer

1¾ cups icing sugar
⅓ cup margarine
½ cup mashed very ripe banana
½ teaspoon vanilla
1½ teaspoons cinnamon

1. In a large bowl mix the sugar, margarine, and banana on medium until combined. Add the vanilla and cinnamon.
2. Mix on medium high until well combined, smooth, and the fat no longer separates.

Icing Sugar

2 cups sugar
½ cup cornstarch or arrowroot starch

1. Blend ingredients in a processor until fine and powdery.

Chocolate Jelly Roll

YIELD: 8 SLICES OF CAKE

Parchment Paper

1 cup soymilk
3 teaspoons powdered agar
pinch of turmeric
1 cup flour
¼ cup cocoa
1 teaspoon baking powder
½ teaspoon cream of tartar
⅔ cup sugar
⅓ cup + 2 tablespoons margarine
1 tablespoon vanilla
½ cup + 2 tablespoons water
Creem Topping (page 91)

1. Cut parchment paper and place on baking sheet with short sides. In a small pot mix the soymilk, agar, and turmeric. Simmer on medium low until thick then cool.
2. In a small bowl mix the flour, cocoa, baking powder, and cream of tartar. In a large bowl cream the sugar, margarine, and vanilla.
3. Mix water into agar mixture. Alternate flour and agar mixture into creamed margarine. Pour onto baking sheet and level off so it's even. Bake 350° F about 30 minutes.
4. When cool spread lots of creem topping on the cake and then roll up carefully lengthwise to look like a jelly roll. Sift some icing sugar on top.

There's turmeric in this recipe in case you want to make a yellow cake. Just omit the cocoa.

Give It a Rest Chocolate Brownies

YIELD: AN 8-INCH PAN

So you've tried some things in this book and your roommates are on the verge of getting diabetes from all your concoctions — slow down! This recipe, adapted from the Double Chocolate Fudge Brownies in Great Good Desserts Naturally *by Fran Costigan, is rich, tasty, and healthy. It is quite remarkable how yummy it is without wheat or a lot of sweetener. Bake for a couple minutes less if you want the center gooey.*

1½ cup mixed wheat-free flour (ie. spelt, barley, brown rice)
¾ cup cocoa or ⅔ cup cocoa plus 2 tablespoons malt powder
1¼ teaspoons baking powder
¼ teaspoon baking soda
pinch of salt
½ cup maple syrup
½ cup fat substitute (½ cup applesauce or ½ cup pureed prunes work well)
½ cup soymilk
¼ cup oil
1 teaspoon vanilla
1 teaspoon liquid stevia
¼ teaspoon almond extract
½ cup grain sweetened chocolate chips

1. Preheat oven to 350° F. Grease an 8-inch pan.
2. In a large bowl mix the dry ingredients, except for the chocolate chips, and stir with a whisk.
3. In a small bowl whisk the wet ingredients until frothy. Quickly stir the wet into the dry and mix in the chocolate chips. Pour into pan.
4. Bake for about 18 minutes. Set on a wire rack to cool. Depending on the flour you use you might have to cool completely before removing from pan. Finer flour like rice breaks apart easily when warm.

Better For Ya Chocolate Chip Cookies

YIELD: ABOUT 24

A crispy soft sweet cookie without "bad" sugar.

Parchment paper

3 cups gluten–free flour (ie. sorghum, millet, rice)
1 teaspoon baking soda
1 teaspoon baking powder
½ cup oil
½ cup brown rice syrup
½ cup + 2 tablespoons maple syrup
2 teaspoons vanilla
½ cup grain sweetened chocolate chips

1. Preheat oven to 350° F. Oil one or two baking sheets well.
2. In a large bowl mix the dry ingredients except for the chocolate chips.
3. In a small bowl whisk the wet ingredients until frothy. Mix the wet into the dry. Form balls and flatten slightly on baking sheet.
4. Bake for about 12 minutes. Let cool for a minute, then loosen from sheet. Cool a few minutes more then remove from pan. Store in an airtight container, putting wax paper between layers.

Baking on parchment paper is a good choice for this recipe as the syrups make them stick to the baking sheet as they cool.

Chocolate Malt Cookies

YIELD: 9 LARGE COOKIES

This is a chocolate malt recipe for all you who can't find barley malt powder.

⅔ cup flour
¼ cup cocoa
¼ baking powder
1 cup sugar
3 tablespoons margarine
3 tablespoons malt syrup
2 teaspoons oil
1 teaspoon vanilla
2½ tablespoons mini chips or chopped chocolate

1. Grease baking sheet and preheat oven to 325° F.
2. In a medium bowl mix the flour, cocoa, and baking powder.
2. In a large bowl mix the sugar, margarine, malt, oil, and vanilla.
3. Mix the dry into the wet and add chocolate. Squeeze with hands to form a dough ball.
4. Break off 9 balls and press down on pan. Bake for 15–20 minutes.

Peanut Butter Brownies

YIELD: AN 8–INCH PAN

2 ounces unsweetened chocolate
⅓ cup natural peanut butter
¼ cup oil
2 tablespoons ground flaxseed mixed with 6 tablespoons water
½ cup + 3 tablespoons flour
1¼ cups brown sugar, lightly packed
⅓ cup walnuts

1. Melt the chocolate in a double boiler (or medium pot over a larger pot of simmering water.) Mix in the peanut butter, oil and flax mixture.
2. Preheat oven to 325° F.
3. In a large bowl mix the flour and sugar. Mix wet into dry and pour into greased 8–inch pan. Pat walnuts on top and bake for 30 minutes.

Peanut Butter Pie

YIELD: AN 8- OR 9–INCH PIE

Syrupy chocolate and heavy creamy peanut butter make this an excellent dessert.

2 cups natural peanut butter
1 – 1½ cup icing sugar
½ pound firm tofu
1 tablespoon lemon juice
⅛ – ¼ teaspoon salt
2½ cups Creem Topping (make with ½ tsp agar!) (page 91)
½ cup chocolate sauce (page 127)
1 pie crust — any type, prebaked if needed

1. Blend the first 5 ingredients. Pour into a large bowl and fold in creem topping.
2. Pour a little over ¼ cup of chocolate sauce onto the bottom of the pie crust. Pour filling. Drizzle about 2 more tablespoons of chocolate sauce on top.
3. Chill for a couple hours until set and then nibble away at this scrumptious, rich dessert.

Chocolate Sauce

YIELD: ABOUT 2 CUPS

3 tablespoons maple syrup
¾ cup soymilk
3 teaspoons arrowroot
1½ cups chocolate chips

1. In a small bowl mix the maple syrup, soymilk, and arrowroot.
2. Melt the chocolate chips in a double boiler (or smaller pot on top of a larger pot of simmering water.) Add the rest of the ingredients, stirring quickly. Stir on direct low heat until thick.

Nanaimo Bars

YIELD: 8–INCH PAN

Nanaimo is a town on Vancouver Island, and when I was there I insisted on eating one of these squares. Very rich — you only need a little piece.

First Layer:
½ cup margarine
¼ cup sugar
5 tablespoons cocoa
1¼ cup ground animal crackers
1 cup coconut
2 tablespoons ground flaxseed mixed with 3 tablespoons water

1. In a medium pot melt the margarine, sugar, and cocoa.
2. Add the animal crackers and coconut and mix well. Add the flax mixture.
3. Press into a greased 8–inch pan. Chill.

Second Layer:
2 cups icing sugar
½ cup margarine
2 tablespoons custard powder
2 tablespoons soymilk

1. In a medium bowl cream all together and spread over chocolate crust.

Topping:
½ cup chocolate chips
2 tablespoons margarine

1. In a small pot melt together over low heat. Spread evenly on second layer. Chill.

Sweetened Condensed Soymilk

YIELD: 3½ CUPS

2½ cup boiling water
1 cup soymilk powder
⅔ cup sugar
3 tablespoons margarine, melted
¼ teaspoon lemon juice

1. Combine ingredients in a blender in order, blending each time, until smooth. Refrigerate.

Chocolate Brownie Cheezecake

YIELD: 2 9–INCH CHEESECAKES

Brownies and cheezecake combined? No, you are not dreaming!
It's a stomach ache in a pie tin if you're not careful.

Brownie:
3 unsweetened squares of chocolate (3 ounces)
⅓ cup margarine
1¼ cup sugar
½ cup flour
1 teaspoon vanilla
3 tablespoons ground flaxseed mixed with 4 tablespoons water

1. In a large pot melt the chocolate and margarine on medium low heat. Remove from heat and add sugar, flour, and vanilla. Add the egg replacer, mixing well.
2. Pour equally into two greased 9–inch round cake or pie plate.

Cheezecake:
5 squares unsweetened chocolate (5 ounces)
1 tub vegan cream cheese (8 ounces)
¾ cup soy yogurt
1 cup firm tofu
1¾ cups unpacked brown sugar
2 tablespoons cornstarch
¼ cup flour
1 teaspoon vanilla
pinch of salt

1. In a large pot melt the chocolate in a double boiler.
2. In a processor blend all ingredients including chocolate. Pour equally into the two pans with brownie batter.
3. Bake at 325° F for about 50 minutes. Cool.

Spelt–Espresso–Chocolate Chip (The Axis of Evil) Cookies

YIELD: 2 DOZEN COOKIES

AKA Patrick's Perfect Chocolate Chip Cookies. Patrick always complains his cookies are too hard or too soft but they never fail to be completely devoured in nanoseconds at punk shows. And they're made with spelt!

2½ cups of spelt flour
1½ teaspoon of baking powder
1 teaspoon salt
⅔ cup oil
½ cup sugar
½ cup brown sugar
⅓ cup hot espresso (or ⅓ hot water and 1 tablespoon espresso powder)
1 teaspoon vanilla
¾ – 1 cup chocolate chips

1. Preheat oven to 350° F. In a medium bowl combine the flour, baking powder, and salt.
2. In a large bowl mix oil, sugar, and brown sugar. Add espresso and vanilla.
3. Add the flour mixture to the wet mixture and mix well.
4. Add the chocolate chips and continue mixing. Scoop the dough with a spoon, and shape it into a ball. Press the balls down onto a baking sheet with your fingers.
5. Bake for approximately 13 minutes. Let cookies cool for about 10 minutes before removing them from the sheet.

Grandma's Peanut Butter Cookies

YIELD: 12–13 COOKIES

*I don't think my grandma ever put chocolate chips in her yummy,
flavorful cookies, but I think she would approve.*

½ cup natural peanut butter
¼ cup margarine
½ cup brown sugar
½ cup white sugar
2 tablespoons ground flaxseed mixed with 4 tablespoons water
1¼ cups flour
1 teaspoon baking soda
pinch of salt
½ cup chocolate chips

1. Preheat oven to 350° F. Lightly grease a baking sheet.
2. In a large bowl mix the peanut butter and margarine with a fork. Sift sugars into the bowl. Mix.
3. Mix in the flax. Sift in the flour, baking soda, and salt. Mix well. Mix in chocolate chips.
4. Roll dough into balls about the size of walnuts. Place on baking sheet and press down in a criss-cross pattern with a fork. Press well for flatter cookies and lightly for chunkier. Bake 15–20 minutes, depending on how thick the cookies are.

Sweet Potato Chocolate Chip Cookies

YIELD: ABOUT 18 COOKIES

I walked into a health food store and snapped up these cookies right away.
They proved chewy, mouth-watering, and extremely expensive, so I set out to make my own.

¾ cup packed brown sugar
½ cup white sugar
½ cup plus 2 tablespoons margarine
⅓ cup cooked and mashed sweet potato
1 teaspoon vanilla
1½ cups flour
¼ teaspoon baking soda
¼ teaspoon cinnamon
¼ teaspoon allspice
pinch of salt
⅔ cup chocolate chips

1. Preheat oven to 350° F. In a large bowl cream the sugars and margarine well.
2. Add the sweet potato and vanilla and cream well.
3. In a small bowl sift the flour, baking soda, salt, and spices. Add this to the wet ingredients and mixing just until the flour is incorporated. Mix in chocolate chips.
4. Make dough into 18 balls and set on ungreased cookie sheet. Flatten slightly. Bake about 15 minutes or until the bottoms are a caramel brown color.
5. Set cookies on racks to cool, they will set up a bit more before they cool completely.

"But I can't get that!" S'mores

It's hard to find honey-free graham crackers and vegan marshmallows are only available online for most people. This satisfies that S'more craving and is fast.

Some animal crackers
Some Suzanne's Ricemellow Creme (or make your own, page 148)
Some melted chocolate

1. Take an animal cracker, spread with chocolate then marshmallow creem.

Josh's "I support the SHAC 7" Doughnuts

YIELD: ABOUT A 16 DONUTS

The SHAC 7 are six animal rights activists (and an activist organization) who have been jailed for 1–6 years under the United States Federal Animal Enterprise Protection Act. They are the first people convicted under this act that punishes anyone who "physically disrupts" an animal business. What did they do? They allegedly ran a website, attended demonstrations, and gave speeches about Huntingdon Life Sciences — a particularly cruel animal testing facility. Please donate for their appeals and write to them — they would love to hear thoughtful wishes. This is only the first wave; there will be many more people imprisoned if we don't express our outrage. www.shac7.com

1 cup lukewarm water
2 packs yeast
1 tablespoon sugar
4 – 4½ cup spelt pastry or wheat flour
1 teaspoon salt
1 cup soymilk
⅓ cup + 2 tablespoons sugar
¼ cup melted margarine
2 tablespoons potato starch or rice flour
1 teaspoon vanilla
bottle of vegetable oil

1. Put water, yeast, and sugar into a small bowl. This is called "yeast proof" and it is the most important part of the doughnut experience. This will make or break your doughnuts! Mix and set aside to proof for 10 minutes.
2. In a large bowl mix the flour and salt and set aside.
3. In a large bowl mix the soymilk, sugar, margarine, starch or flour, and vanilla.
4. Add the yeast proof mixture to the wet mixture and gradually beat in flour/salt.
5. Beat in flour. Once you are finished you are going to add a tad bit of flour until the mix is stiff, yet sticky. Don't spend too much time on this though, your yeast is rising!
6. Now we do what is called the "first rise" — cover the dough with cloth and place it in an unheated oven for 1 hour.
7. Turn out the dough on floured surface and knead in a tiny bit of flour for 15–30 strokes.

8. Roll out and cut into doughnuts. (Use a large glass, flour the rim). Cover with cloth and allow to rise for 15–30 minutes or until doubled. If your yeast was good and you did the proof right, the doughnuts will visibly grow during this period. While they are rising, you need to get your oil ready. This is the second most important part of the process.

9. Heat oil slowly for 20 minutes. You'll want a deep pan and you should use a whole bottle of vegetable oil. You can test if it is the right temperature (350°–375° degrees) by dropping a small piece of dough into the oil. The temperature is right if it rises almost immediately and turns a golden color in about a minute. If it burns, it's too hot, and if it does not rise from the bottom or just gets mushy with oil then you need more heat.

10. Cook doughnuts — just drop them in and then turn them over after about a minute with a wooden spoon.

11. Take them out of the oil and let them sit on a paper towel or cloth rag.

In order for these doughnuts to qualify in this chocolate and candy cookbook we'll make them into Boston Creem:

Make a batch of vegan custard from a tin of custard powder. When cool, use the end of a wooden spoon and insert into side of doughnuts, wiggling it around. Put custard in icing gun/bag or plastic bag with small hole cut in corner. Squeeze the custard into the doughnut — put as much as you can in there. Feel free to use vanilla or butterscotch pudding for a filling.

Chocolate Glaze:
4 ounces chocolate chips
2 tablespoons margarine
1 teaspoon vanilla
4 cups icing sugar, sifted

1. In a medium pot melt the chocolate and margarine. Add the vanilla. Gradually mix in icing sugar.

Black Bottom Cupcakes

YIELD: 12 CUPCAKES

Yowza. Yet another reason to move to Portland, Oregon, if Lisa will make these for you when you get there. Her baked goods are to die for: www.sweetpeabaking.com.

Mini muffin tin
Electric mixer or whisk

Black Batter:
1 ½ cups flour
1 cup sugar
¼ cup cocoa
1 teaspoon baking soda
½ teaspoon salt
1 cup water
⅓ cup oil
1 tablespoon vinegar
1 teaspoon vanilla

Filling:
8 ounces tofu cream cheese
½ cup sugar
⅛ teaspoon salt
egg replacer equal to one egg (I use about 2 tablespoons silken tofu)
1 cup mini chocolate chips

1. Preheat oven to 350° F.
2. In a large bowl mix all black batter ingredients well with a whisk or electric mixer.
3. In a separate bowl mix the first four filling ingredients, then stir chocolate chips into filling.
4. Grease and flour (flouring is important!) mini muffin tins. Fill tins half full with black batter, then spoon a large teaspoon of filling mixture into each one. Bake for about 8 to 10 minutes. Cool for 10 minutes and dump out of tins.

Triple Chocolate Pudding

YIELD: ABOUT 4 CUPS

When I was in high school I was mad about pudding. It was common for me to eat two cups in one sitting. This is a much richer version of the Chocolate Pudding in my first book, Lickin' the Beaters: Low Fat Vegan Desserts.

1 cup sugar
⅓ cup cocoa, sifted
¼ cup arrowroot
pinch of salt
1½ ounces unsweetened chocolate
3 cups chocolate soymilk
3 tablespoons margarine
2 teaspoons vanilla

1. In a medium pot mix sugar, cocoa, arrowroot, and salt.
2. Chop the chocolate finely.
3. Slowly whisk the soymilk into the pot, making sure there are no lumps.
4. Heat on medium, add chocolate. Stir constantly until chocolate melts and pudding thickens. Let it boil for about one minute and then take off heat.
5. Add the margarine and vanilla mixing well.
6. Eat warm or cold. To prevent "pudding skin," put a piece of plastic wrap on top of the pudding and poke a few holes with a toothpick.

Use ⅓ cup arrowroot for a very thick dessert.

Most Fabulous Chocolate Brownies

YIELD: 8–INCH PAN

*This recipe crossed my path by way of Webly, was inspired by Kittee, and belongs to Shara —
all amazing vegan cooks! Most definitely the best vegan chocolate brownies I've ever eaten!*

1 cup brown sugar

½ cup white sugar

½ cup margarine

4 teaspoons dry egg replacer mixed with 6 tablespoons water

1¼ cups flour

½ cup cocoa

1 teaspoon vanilla

1 teaspoon baking powder

½ teaspoon salt

¾ cup chocolate chips (optional)

¾ cup chopped pecans (optional)

1. Preheat oven to 350° degrees. Grease an 8–inch pan. In a medium bowl cream the sugars, margarine, egg replacer, and vanilla.
2. In a large bowl sift the dry ingredients together and mix.
3. Mix the wet into the dry and bake for about 35 minutes.

Ice Creem Hints

Get an ice cream maker, penny pincher!
I bought two of mine at thrift stores for less than
$10. A new huge maker using ice and a plastic
bucket costs about $20. It really makes a difference.
If you really don't have the money or space then
you can use this method: Blend the ingredients and
pour into a 9 x 13–inch metal pan. Place in freezer
and mix every hour. Eventually, many, many hours
later, it will firm up.

⸙ If you don't like the taste of your soymilk, you
won't like the taste of your ice creem. As you
probably know, some soymilks are "beanier" than
others.

⸙ When putting chunks of things into your ice
creem refrigerate or freeze them and add them at
the last minute. If you put them in at the beginning they will sink to the bottom immediately.

⸙ Usually ice cream finished in a home machine is
about the consistency of soft serve. After you've
run your machine transfer the contents to a
container with a lid and freeze until desired
consistency. Homemade ice cream gets *very* hard
after it sets up in the freezer (although if you
use alcohol based vanilla in these recipes this
shouldn't be a problem). You will have to "ripen"
it in order to eat it.

⸙ "Ripening" just means let it thaw in your fridge
until it is scoopable. Ice cream bought at the store,
vegan and dairy, have agents inside to keep them
scoopable at all times.

⸙ Store in an airtight container that fits the ice
creem well. Frosting happens when there is too
much air in the container. (Although I think these
ice creems will get eaten up long before that!)

⸙ The longer you freeze your blended ingredients
the shorter time it will take in the ice cream
machine.

⸙ Your ice creem will puff up with air as you freeze
it in the maker so don't put any more than $^2/_3$ of
mixture into the freezing canister.

⸙ The ice creem recipes in these book use alcohol-
based flavorings which gives them a perfect
texture. Often, alcohol will prevent your ice
creem from freezing. If you want to make an
alcohol-flavored ice creem (like Margarita) it
will be more of a slush or ice rather than smooth
"creem." If you use glycerine-based flavorings in
these recipes you may find the ice cream becomes
very solid after freezing. Just thaw for a while in
the fridge before eating.

Ice Creem Bon Bons

YIELD: 30 BON BONS

Aluminum foil
Melon ball scooper

2 cups soy ice creem (recipes to follow)
¾ cup chocolate chips
¼ cup margarine
3 tablespoons soymilk

1. Line a baking sheet with foil and freeze for 15 minutes.
2. Scoop the ice cream into small balls and freeze until very firm, about 2 hours. Work fast so the balls don't melt.
3. In a medium pot melt chocolate with margarine and soymilk on low heat. Cool to room temperature.
4. Quickly coat the ice cream balls in chocolate, using two forks or a dipping instrument, and refreeze until firm.

Vanilla Ice Creem

YIELD: ABOUT 2 PINTS

1 ⅔ cups soymilk
⅔ cup sugar
½ cup oil
½ of a 12.3-ounce silken firm tofu package (about ¾ cup)
1 teaspoon vanilla
pinch of salt

1. Blend the soymilk, sugar, oil, tofu, vanilla, and salt. Chill for at least 2 hours.
2. Freeze according to your ice cream maker instructions.

Eat plain or use as a base for these gourmet flavors. Add the extras in just before ice cream is ready. Experiment with quantity as some folks like their ice cream chunkier than others.

Cherry Cheezecake Ice Creem

YIELD: ABOUT 2½ PINTS

½ cup chopped animal crackers
½ cup halved canned cherries (drained well, set juice aside)
5 tablespoons sugar
½ tub tofu cream cheese (4 ounces)
2 tablespoons lemon juice
2 teaspoons arrowroot or cornstarch

1. Refrigerate animal crackers and cherries while preparing and making ice creem. Freeze a large cake pan.
2. Use only ½ the tofu in the original recipe. Add 3 tablespoons sugar, tofu cream cheese, and lemon juice to the ice cream while you are blending.
3. In a pot, whisk the canned cherry juice with 2 tablespoons sugar and 2 teaspoons arrowroot. There should be about ¾ cup of cherry juice. If not, add extra fruit juice. Simmer until thick and then put into freezer to make very cold.
4. Add the animal crackers and cherries to the ice cream just before its ready. Pour into frozen cake pan. Quickly pour the cold cherry juice on top and zig-zag gently in using a spatula or knife. Don't mix too much or you will lose the cherry ribbon.

Che-rry Guevara Ice Creem

Some people like to name their ice creems after aging hippies. I prefer revolutionaries.

⅓ cup halved cherries (fresh or from can, drained well)
⅓ cup shaved semisweet chocolate (freeze chocolate bar and
grate with cheese grater or carrot peeler)

1. Refrigerate the chocolate and cherries while preparing and making ice creem.

Chocolate Chip Cookie Dough Ice Creem

⅔ cup raw cookie dough chunks, small

1. Freeze the dough on a plate so chunks aren't touching.

Chocolate Chip Ice Creem

⅔ cup mini semisweet chocolate chips

1. Refrigerate the chocolate chips while preparing and making ice creem. Replace vanilla with 1 teaspoon mint extract to make Mint Chocolate Chip.

Chips and Chunks Ice Creem

⅓ cup Butterscotch Fudge chunks, small chunks (page 21)
⅓ cup chopped chocolate chips

1. Freeze the fudge on a plate so chunks aren't touching. Refrigerate the chips.

Honee Banana Caramel Swirl Ice Creem

⅓ cup Honee Banana Caramel (page 41)

1. Melt the caramel a bit so it is thin enough to drop quickly from a spoon. Spoon it in your ice creem and mix slightly.

Chocolate Ice Creem

YIELD: ABOUT 2 PINTS

2 ounces unsweetened chocolate
1 ⅔ cups soymilk
⅓ cup cocoa
¾ cup sugar
⅓ cup oil
½ cup silken tofu
1 teaspoon vanilla
pinch of salt

1. Melt the chocolate in a double boiler (or a medium size pot on top of a large pot of simmering water.)
2. Mix in the soymilk and whisk in the cocoa. Add the sugar and simmer for a couple minutes, stirring constantly.
3. Blend with oil, tofu, vanilla, and salt.
4. Freeze in ice cream maker.

Eat plain or use as a base for the gourmet flavors that follow. Add the extras in just before ice cream is ready. Experiment with quantity, as some folks like their ice creem chunkier than others.

Chocolate Fudge Chunk Ice Creem

⅓ cup Chocolate Fudge chunks, small (page 22)

1. Freeze the fudge on a plate so chunks aren't touching.

Chocolate Orange Ice Creem

3 tablespoons frozen orange juice concentrate

1. Add the juice concentrate with the other blended ingredients.

Chocolate Candied Nuts Ice Creem

⅓ cup chopped candied nuts (many recipes in this book)

Chocolate Coconut Ice Creem

⅓ cup unsweetened shredded coconut

1. Place coconut on a baking sheet and toast in a 300° F oven until it begins to tan. Stir every once in a while until toasted to your liking. Fry with a little bit of oil for richer, crispier coconut.

Mocha Ice Creem

2 tablespoons freeze-dried coffee

1. Add the coffee as you blend the ingredients.

Rocky Road Ice Creem

YIELD: 1 PINT

This one is very rich, but you'll keep going back to it for just a little more.

4 tablespoons toasted walnuts
4 tablespoons chopped marshmallow (page 148)
2 tablespoons mini chocolate chips (or minced chocolate)
4 ounces unsweetened chocolate
1 ½ cups milk
1 ½ cups Creem Topping (page 91)
1 cup sugar
1 teaspoon vanilla
pinch of salt

1. Place the walnuts, marshmallow, and mini chocolate chips in separate bowls and freeze.
2. Melt the chocolate in a double boiler (or a small pot on top of a bigger pot of simmering water.) Blend the milk, creem topping, sugar, vanilla, and salt.
3. When chocolate is melted pour ½ of the blender mixture into it and mix well. Pour this chocolate mix into the rest of the blender mixture and blend well.
4. Freeze according to your ice cream maker. When the mixture is the texture of soft ice cream add the cold walnuts, marshmallow, and chocolate chips.

S'more Ice Creem

YIELD: 1 PINT

Marshmallow:
¾ cup sugar
½ cup water
½ cup corn syrup
dash of salt
1 teaspoon agar powder
1 tablespoon vanilla
cornstarch for dusting

Ice Creem:
¾ cup minced graham crackers
⅓ cup minced chocolate
1 cup firm tofu
1 ½ cups soymilk
4 teaspoons blackstrap molasses
2 tablespoons rice syrup
½ cups sugar
2 teaspoons vanilla
4 tablespoons oil

1. First make the marshmallow: mix first 5 ingredients in medium pot and boil. Remove from heat and blend in mixing bowl with an electric mixer for 15 minutes. This incorporates air and fluffs it up. Add vanilla just before finishing. Pour into an 8-inch pan. Allow to cool fully. Coat the slab of marshmallow with cornstarch and store in an airtight container at room temperature. For this recipe, coat 4 tablespoons of chopped marshmallows with cornstarch and set aside.
2. Chill the graham crackers and chocolate.
3. Blend the tofu, soymilk, molasses, rice syrup, sugar, vanilla, and oil. Freeze in ice cream maker.
4. Just before the ice cream is finished add the crackers and chocolate.
5. Remove the paddle from the ice cream maker and gently fold in the marshmallow pieces.

For 11 years I have been trying to make good vegan marshmallows. I admit defeat in the area of fluffiness. Just not the same. If you can find some professional vegan marshmallows, skip the homemade recipe. If you'd rather have a swirl of marshmallow creem cut down agar powder to ¼ teaspoon and mix for 5 minutes. Gently fold ¼ cup into the ice creem at the end.

Biographies

Siue Moffat puts things on paper and film. She loves making vegan candy (check out her new company — *www.BoardwalkChocolates.com*) and inspecting beat-up film collections. Radical politics make her eyes light up and Peanuts comics make her giggle. Siue lives here and there (currently Toronto) and has a love/hate relationship with sugar and punk rock. *www.dairyfreedesserts.com* / *beaterlicker@yahoo.com*

Celso grew up in Boulder, Colorado, but now lives in Portland, Oregon, where he works as a caretaker and writes his comic *Monk in Ogreland*. He has done work in zines such as, *Celso, Free, Hame-Kame-Ha!* and *Clip-Tart*. Although he can't commune with inter-dimensional beings, he often pretends he can and convinces others that this is so. *celso333@hotmail.com*

Missy Kulik For over half her life Missy Kulik has been a self-publisher. Her background is focused in graphic design, but her first love is art. Missy works as a product and graphic designer by day, but by night she draws comics for the free weekly paper called *Flagpole Magazine*. In her spare time she enjoys sewing, baking, drawing, and studying trapeze. She lives in a very cute house with Raoul and her cat, Nilla in Athens, Georgia. *www.Missykulik.com*

Index

About PM Press

PM Press was founded at the end of 2007 by a small collection of folks with decades of publishing, media, and organizing experience. PM Press co-conspirators have published and distributed hundreds of books, pamphlets, CDs, and DVDs. Members of PM have founded enduring book fairs, spearheaded victorious tenant organizing campaigns, and worked closely with bookstores, academic conferences, and even rock bands to deliver political and challenging ideas to all walks of life. We're old enough to know what we're doing and young enough to know what's at stake.

We seek to create radical and stimulating fiction and non-fiction books, pamphlets, t-shirts, visual and audio materials to entertain, educate, and inspire you. We aim to distribute these through every available channel with every available technology — whether that means you are seeing anarchist classics at our bookfair stalls; reading our latest vegan cookbook at the café; downloading geeky fiction e-books; or digging new music and timely videos from our website.

PM Press is always on the lookout for talented and skilled volunteers, artists, activists and writers to work with. If you have a great idea for a project or can contribute in some way, please get in touch.

About Tofu Hound Press

Tofu Hound Press is a small independent publisher with a commitment to publishing quality books on veganism, vegan cooking, animal rights, and related issues. We're small, but we have a lot of heart, and we work hard to bring valuable, vital, entertaining, and useful titles to market. Our goal is to publish smaller runs of books that otherwise might not make it to market through conventional publishers. We're just a few like-minded folks who want to get important ideas out there that might not see the light of day because of their limited profitability. For us profitable ideas aren't always the best ones, and we refuse to limit ourselves to the least common denominator in what we write and publish.

We're small and agile enough that we can exist in the spaces between the giants. In fact, we think that's where most of the exciting stuff is happening. We dig independent media. To the greatest extent possible, we work with people who share our values. If what we publish can make even the tiniest of difference, we've accomplished what we've set out to accomplish.

Starting in 2010, some of our titles will be published as an imprint of PM Press.

Tofu Hound Press was founded in 2005, and named for the two dogs who come running every time they hear us open a package of tofu. Of course we oblige, and think of it as an inexpensive royalty for using their story as our name.

Find out more at www.tofuhoundpress.com.

Friends of PM Press

These are indisputably momentous times — the financial system is melting down globally and the Empire is stumbling. Now more than ever there is a vital need for radical ideas.

In the three years since its founding — and on a mere shoestring — PM Press has risen to the formidable challenge of publishing and distributing knowledge and entertainment for the struggles ahead. With over 100 releases to date, we have published an impressive and stimulating array of literature, art, music, politics, and culture. Using every available medium, we've succeeded in connecting those hungry for ideas and information to those putting them into practice.

Friends of PM allows you to directly help impact, amplify, and revitalize the discourse and actions of radical writers, filmmakers, and artists. It provides us with a stable foundation from which we can build upon our early successes and provides a much-needed subsidy for the materials that can't necessarily pay their own way. You can help make that happen — and receive every new title automatically delivered to your door once a month — by joining as a Friend of PM Press. And, we'll throw in a free T-Shirt when you sign up.

Here are your options:

- $25 a month: Get all books and pamphlets plus 50% discount on all webstore purchases

- $25 a month: Get all CDs and DVDs plus 50% discount on all webstore purchases

- $40 a month: Get all PM Press releases plus 50% discount on all webstore purchases

- $100 a month: Superstar — Everything plus PM merchandise, free downloads, and 50% discount on all webstore purchases

For those who can't afford $25 or more a month, we're introducing Sustainer Rates at $15, $10 and $5. Sustainers get a free PM Press t-shirt and a 50% discount on all purchases from our website.

Your Visa or Mastercard will be billed once a month, until you tell us to stop. Or until our efforts succeed in bringing the revolution around. Or the financial meltdown of Capital makes plastic redundant. Whichever comes first.

More information at www.pmpress.org — click on the Friends of PM link.